Books by Dan Carlinsky

A Century of College Humor:
Cartoons, Stories, Poems, Jokes &
Assorted Foolishness from over 95
Campus Magazines

The Complete Bible Quiz Book

Typewriter Art

The Great 1960s Quiz

with Edwin Goodgold

Trivia

More Trivial Trivia

Rock 'n' Roll Trivia

The Compleat Beatles Quiz Book

The World's Greatest Monster Quiz

with David Heim

Bicycle Tours in and Around New
York

The Great 1960s Quiz

by Dan Carlinsky

Harper & Row, Publishers

New York, Hagerstown,
San Francisco,
London

THE GREAT 1960S QUIZ. Copyright © 1978 by Dan Carlinsky. All rights reserved. Printed in the United States of America. No part of this book may be used or reproduced in any manner whatsoever without written permission except in the case of brief quotations embodied in critical articles and reviews. For information address Harper & Row, Publishers, Inc., 10 East 53rd Street, New York, N.Y. 10022. Published simultaneously in Canada by Fitzhenry & Whiteside Limited, Toronto.

First Edition

Designed by Stephanie Tevonian

Library of Congress Cataloging in Publication Data

Carlinsky, Dan.
    The great 1960s quiz.
    1. United States—History—1961–1969—Miscellanea.
I. Title.
E841.C28 1978 973.92 77–11817
ISBN 0–06–090646–4 pbk.

78 79 80 81 82 10 9 8 7 6 5 4 3 2 1

America in the Sixties was pushing 200, but politically the nation was in its midlife crisis. Morally, it was going through puberty. Television and rock music, barely born, were in adolescence—with all the pimples, heartaches, and confusion that stage implies. There were strains all around.

Now it's done. We survived.

Is it too soon to remember the Sixties? No—not for the generation that came of age then. If you were born in the late Forties or Fifties, your nostalgia lies in the Sixties. No "Mairzy Doats" and Fibber McGee for you: the Kennedy assassination, Dr. Kildare, the Beatles, and the Chicago 7 are the New Trivia.

For a while, forget how crucial the decade was. Just remember that you were there. This is the final exam: a lighthearted but comprehensive test on the places and faces, the doings and brewings, from 1960 through 1969.

Have fun. Aren't you sorry you didn't take notes?
—Dan Carlinsky

Many individuals encouraged me and helped me make it through the Sixties for the second time, for which I say a special thanks: Nancy Carlinsky, Bob Cochnar, Elaine Dommu, Tom Dorris, Michael J. Eschelbacher, Rheba Flegelman, Erwin Glikes, Dave Hendin, Peter Janovsky, Fred Knubel, Jill Lesko, Pepper O'Brien, Janet Tara, Walter Wager, Maron Waxman, and Nach Waxman.—*D. C.*

Contents

How to Figure Your Score.   xi-xii

1. Who? 1
2. What? 4
3. Where? 5
4. Why? 7
5. When? 8
6. Dates 9
7. Salutes 10
8. Who Came Before? 10
9. Phrasemaking 11
10. Slogan Power! 12
11. It Pays to Increase Your Word Power 13
12. Compare and Contrast . . . 14
13. And One to Throw You for a Loop 15
14. High Fashion . . . and Low 16
15. Glorious Food 17
16. Memorable Marriages . . . 18
17. Television 20
18. Philosophy and Faith . . . 23
19. If You Can't Answer This One, the Whole Decade Was a Waste 24
20. Alphabet 25
21. A/K/A 25
22. The Movies 26
23. Super Bonus Question in Arithmetic Agility 31
24. The Story of Spiro 31
25. Music: Take 25 32
26. The Letter N 35

27. Complete the Quote 35
28. Campaign Stuff 36
29. True or False? 38
30. In the Middle 39
31. Rivers and Islands 40
32. On Stage 41
33. Vowel Play 42
34. ID, Please 42
35. Sports 43
36. Ha-Ha-Ha 46
37. The Number Game 48
38. Isn't That Whatsisname? . 49
39. Who Died? 51
40. How Did They Die? 53
41. Forgery Identification . . . 54
42. Books 55
43. Initials 56
44. Giant Sixties Word Find . 56
45. What's My Line? 58
46. The Letter X 59
47. Magazines 59
48. A Smattering of Crime . 60
49. What's Happening? 61
50. About Women 64
51. Hidden Words 66
52. Friendly Animals 67
53. Music: Take 20 More . . . 68
54. Colors 70
55. Strikes, Protests, Riots, Etc. 71
56. Words from Our Sponsors 72

57. What Do They Have in Common? 73
58. The Supreme Test 74
59. Who Said? 75
60. One Little Word 79
61. ING 80
62. Quick Associations 81
63. Author! Author! 82
64. Openers 83
65. About Names 84
66. Assassination Minutiae . . 87
67. Song Fragments 88
68. A Half Quiz 88
69. Black Studies 89
70. Fill in the Blanks 91
71. Talk to the Stars 92
72. In a Family Way 94
73. More Sports—for the Hardcore 95
74. Explain 97
75. Just Eyes 98
76. Special Mystery Photo . . .100
77. A Hairy Test 100
78. Health and Welfare 102
79. Multiple Choice 103
80. Odd One Out 107
81. And Then They Grew Up .109
82. Farewells 111
83. The Honors Test 113
84. But 116
85. For High Honors 117
86. Final Potpourri 119

Answers 123

How to Figure Your Score

Including extra credit questions, this book contains a total of 11,940 points. Figure your score on the line provided after each quiz. Total your quiz scores below, and then check with the **How Do You Rate?** table on page xiii. Don't feel bad if you're not at the top of the scale; perhaps your talents lie elsewhere.

1. Who? _____
2. What? _____
3. Where? _____
4. Why? _____
5. When? _____
6. Dates _____
7. Salutes _____
8. Who Came Before? _____
9. Phrasemaking _____
10. Slogan Power! _____
11. It Pays to Increase Your Word Power _____
12. Compare and Contrast _____
13. And One to Throw You for a Loop _____
14. High Fashion . . . and Low _____
15. Glorious Food _____
16. Memorable Marriages _____
17. Television _____
18. Philosophy and Faith _____
19. If You Can't Answer This One, the Whole Decade Was a Waste _____
20. Alphabet _____
21. A/K/A _____
22. The Movies _____
23. Super Bonus Question in Arithmetic Agility _____
24. The Story of Spiro _____
25. Music: Take 25 _____
26. The Letter N _____
27. Complete the Quote _____
28. Campaign Stuff _____
29. True or False? _____
30. In the Middle _____
31. Rivers and Islands _____
32. On Stage _____
33. Vowel Play _____
34. ID, Please _____
35. Sports _____
36. Ha-Ha-Ha _____
37. The Number Game _____
38. Isn't That Whatsisname? _____
39. Who Died? _____
40. How Did They Die? _____
41. Forgery Identification _____
42. Books _____
43. Initials _____
44. Giant Sixties Word Find _____
45. What's My Line? _____
46. The Letter X _____
47. Magazines _____
48. A Smattering of Crime _____
49. What's Happening? _____
50. About Women _____

51. Hidden Words _____

52. Friendly Animals _____

53. Music: Take 20 More _____

54. Colors _____

55. Strikes, Protests, Riots, Etc. _____

56. Words from Our Sponsors _____

57. What Do They Have in Common? _____

58. The Supreme Test _____

59. Who Said? _____

60. One Little Word _____

61. ING _____

62. Quick Associations _____

63. Author! Author! _____

64. Openers _____

65. About Names _____

66. Assassination Minutiae _____

67. Song Fragments _____

68. A Half Quiz _____

69. Black Studies _____

70. Fill in the Blanks _____

71. Talk to the Stars _____

72. In a Family Way _____

73. More Sports—for the Hardcore _____

74. Explain _____

75. Just Eyes _____

76. Special Mystery Photo _____

77. A Hairy Test _____

78. Health and Welfare _____

79. Multiple Choice _____

80. Odd One Out _____

81. And Then They Grew Up _____

82. Farewells _____

83. The Honors Test _____

84. But . . . _____

85. For High Honors _____

86. Final Potpourri _____

Who the Hell Was? _____
(see instructions on page 145)

Grand Total _____

How Do You Rate?

11,940: Either you're a terrible cheat or you know too much for your own good.

11,000–11,939: Magnificent!

9,000–10,999: Very fine.

5,000–8,999: You pass.

3,000–4,999: You weren't paying attention, were you?

1,000–2,999: Hang your head.

less than 1,000: You are obviously under 18 years old or a recent immigrant.

1
Who?

1. . . . was the first human in space?

2. . . . was the first Peace Corps director?

3. . . . played Tom Jones?

4. . . . was the Gray Wizard in Tolkien's *Lord of the Rings?*

5. . . . used the slogan "I can do more for Massachusetts" and won?

6. . . . was the lone dissenting judge in the 1962 Supreme Court decision striking down a state-written prayer from New York schools?

7. . . . issued a statement titled *Pacem in terris?*

8. . . . called TV a "wasteland"?

9. . . . embarrassed the Johnson administration with his men's room activities?

10. . . . became a night club and recording smash imitating JFK?

11. . . . tore through the streets de-Westernizing China by cutting long hair, attacking churches, closing "luxury" shops, and such?

12. . . . gave the smash Black and White Ball in New York, the gala social event of 1966, with 540 celebrities in attendance? (Ten points extra credit if you know who the host's date was.)

13

14

13. . . . was the probable successor to Nehru but lost everything because of a Chinese invasion of India?

14. . . . integrated the state university at Oxford, Miss., in September 1962?

15. . . . was the draft resistance leader better known as one of the top-selling authors of all time?

16. . . . gave a giant aluminum lipstick tube on a caterpillar tread to Yale?

17. . . . was Yale's famous antiwar chaplain?

18. . . . had to fight off flocks of Hitchcock-directed birds?

16

17

18

19. . . . ran the League for Spiritual Discovery?

20. . . . manufactured napalm?

Maybe the initials will help with these questions. Who . . .

21. . . . lent his name to an important report on racism in America? (O. K.)

22. . . . was often cited with amusement for his 1959 prediction, "The employers will love this generation. They aren't going to press many grievances. They are going to be easy to handle. There aren't going to be any riots"? (C. K.)

23. . . . was confronted by a tough Adlai Stevenson in the UN during the Cuban missile crisis? (V. Z.)

24. . . . defected from a Leningrad performing group on a Western tour in 1961? (R. N.)

25. . . . made a trip "on behalf of peace among men"? (He went by jet—the first person in his position ever to fly; P.)

19

23

28

26. . . . was censured by his colleagues in the Senate for his use of campaign funds? (A Connecticut Democrat; T. D.) (Ten points extra credit: Who first aired his doings in the press?)

27. . . . proposed a "war crimes tribunal" in Stockholm but was too ill to attend? (B. R.)

28. . . . was jokingly called "the song-and-dance man" when he successfully ran for a U.S. Senate seat in California? (G. M.)

29. . . . was head of the Merry Pranksters? (K. K.)

30. . . . labeled *Homo sapiens* "the naked ape"? (D. M.)

SCORE＿＿＿× **10 points each** +

＿＿＿ **extra** = ＿＿＿ **(max. 320)**

2
What?

1. . . . happened to Mr. and Mrs. Andrew Fischer of Aberdeen, S.D., on Sept. 14, 1963?

2. . . . did Atlanta do to Milwaukee in 1966?

3. . . . happened to *Thresher* in 1963 and *Scorpion* in 1968?

4. . . . happened to Maria Callas in 1965?

5. . . . did Polaroid do in 1963?

6. . . . happened to Paul Hornung and Alex Karras in 1963?

7. . . . happened to dimes and quarters in 1965?

8. . . . did Julie Andrews and Carol Burnett do in 1962?

9. . . . was done to Adam Clayton Powell in 1967 that hadn't been done to a congressman in 46 years?

10. . . . happened to St. Christopher in 1969?

11. . . . did Lynda Lee Mead of Natchez, Miss., do to Nancy Anne Fleming of Montague, Mich., in 1960?

12. . . . happened to Lloyd M. Bucher in 1968?

13. . . . happened to the U.S.S. *Triton* in 1960?

◀14. . . . happened to this car in 1961?

15. . . . happened to Yale and Vassar in 1968?

SCORE_____ × **10 points each =**

_____**(max. 150)**

14

● WHO THE HELL WAS DANIEL BURROS?

3
Where?

1. Where was Adolf Eichmann captured?

2. In what town did Woodstock take place?

3. Where is Sproul Plaza?

4. The theme was Man in the Space Age. Nine million people showed up. Where?

5. American Nazi leader George Lincoln Rockwell was shot in a shopping center in
   - **A.** Dunn, N.C.
   - **B.** Augusta, Ga.
   - **C.** Holyoke, Mass.
   - **D.** Hempstead, N.Y.
   - **E.** Arlington, Va.

6. Where did Member of Parliament Bernadette Devlin riot, leading to her arrest?

7. The 1960 winter Olympics were the first held in the United States since 1932. Where were they?

8. Can you locate Lincoln Park, People's Park, and Thompson Square Park? (No credit unless you name every city.)

9. One or more bombs went off in the Sixteenth Street Baptist Church while Sunday school was in session. Four girls were killed, 15 other injuries were reported. The year was 1963. Where?

10. Where did Governor George Wallace "stand in the schoolhouse door"?

11. What was the suburban Connecticut town made famous for a teenage drinking problem?

12. _____ 4 was one of several hamlets that made up the village of Song My in the province of Quang Nga. For quite a while it was the most talked-about hamlet in the world. Name it.

13. The 1962 TV show *It's a Man's World* put a bunch of kids into a strange kind of house. The setting didn't work—the show was canceled. But what kind of place was it?

14. An incident during the 1967 Detroit riots became the subject of an important Sixties book by John Hersey. Where did this incident take place?

15. Where did the CIA train anti-Castro troops for the Bay of Pigs invasion?

    A. Miami
    B. Orlando
    C. New Orleans
    D. Guatemala
    E. Jamaica

16. Complete this phrase: "Beautiful downtown _____."

17. Name the motel in which Anthony Perkins stabbed Janet Leigh in *Psycho.*

18. With whom do you identify these places: Blue Jay Way, Bishopsgate, the Isle of Wight?

19. What was the name of LBJ's ranch in Texas?

20. This Texas place opened in April 1965. It cost $31.6 million to build, including air conditioning. President Johnson was there for the opening. So were the New York Yankees. Is that enough of a clue?

21. A 1966 song hit by the New Vaudeville Band told about an English landmark. Name it.

22. In 1961 they renamed it the Grand Ole Opry House. What was it before?

23. When this lady wasn't playing with her umbrella, she was employed by the Banks family at   ▼

    A. 79 Wistful Vista
    B. 77 Sunset Strip
    C. 17 Cherry Tree Lane
    D. 221-B Baker Street
    E. 1313 Blueview Terrace

25

24. What was the original name of JFK International Airport?

25. Where did Johnson and Kosygin hold their 1967 summit?

SCORE _____ × **10 points each =**

_____ **(max. 250)**

17

23

● WHO THE HELL WAS MAX YASGUR?

4
Why?

1. "This is John Chancellor, some-where in custody." Why?

2. In 1967 smart folks were keeping their eyes open for a certain kind of $1 bill. What kind and why?

3. For five years this man ran from the law. Why?▶

4. Selective Service reclassified Cassius Clay 1-A in 1967. Earlier, he had been deferred. Why?

5. No one could argue the fact that *The Virginian* was really different from all other TV westerns. Why? (Ten points extra credit for giving the Virginian's job, and ten points more for naming the place he worked.)

SCORE_____× 10 points each +

_____extra =_____(max. 70)

● WHO THE HELL WAS REGIS PHILBIN?

5
When?

In what year did

1. . . . civil rights marchers and state troopers battle in Selma, Ala.?

2. . . . Roger Maris hit 61 home runs?

3. . . . Martin Luther King receive the Nobel Peace Prize?

4. . . . Pope Paul visit the United States?

5. . . . France resign from NATO?

6. Ten of these events occurred in the Sixties. Pick them. (Score each item as one question.)

   A. Cyclamate ban was announced

   B. Caryl Chessman was executed

   C. Starvation spread in Biafra

   D. Khrushchev visited the U.S.A.

   E. King Kong battled Godzilla

   F. *Ma Perkins* and *Young Doctor Malone* went off the air

   G. *Folk Medicine* hit the bestseller lists

   H. Walter Cronkite took over the *CBS Evening News*

4

61

   I. Algeria gained independence

   J. The Bank of America branch at Santa Barbara was burned

   K. Zip Code started

   L. S. I. Hayakawa became president of San Francisco State College

   M. Willy Brandt became chancellor of West Germany

SCORE_____ **× 10 points each =**

_____ **(max. 150)**

● WHO THE HELL WAS CARL OGLESBY?

6
Dates

Pick the date on the right that fits the event on the left. You know more than you think. With some careful deduction you can probably get them all.

1. Moratorium Day   Aug. 29, 1966

2. Tet Offensive   Jan. 29, 1968

3. Beatles' last American concert   Mar. 31, 1968

4. First moon walk   Oct. 15, 1969

5. President Johnson's no-run announcement   July 20, 1969

SCORE_____ × **10 points each** = _____**(max. 50)**

7
Salutes

1. The most famous salute of the Sixties was given at a funeral. By whom?

2. The decade's *second* most famous salute was an impolite middle-finger thrust by comic Jackie Mason. Where?

3. Speaking of that particular breed of gesture, a young boy gave the same in *Putney Swope.* What made things worse was the object of his salute. Remember who?

4. What celebrated news photo showed American military officers subtly extending middle fingers?

5. Describe the Vulcan Salute. (Ten points extra credit if you know the appropriate accompanying blessing.)

SCORE_____ × **10 points each** +

_____**extra** = _____**(max. 60)**

8
Who Came Before?

1. . . . Lester B. Pearson as Canadian prime minister?

2. . . . John Gronouski as postmaster general?

3. . . . Indira Gandhi as prime minister of India?

4. . . . John Chancellor as host of the *Today* show?

5. . . . Henry Cabot Lodge as chief U.S. Vietnam peace negotiator in Paris?

SCORE_____ × **10 points** = _____

(max. 50)

● WHO THE HELL WAS MARIO SAVIO?

9
Phrasemaking

Certain phrases of the Sixties should come trippingly to your tongue. Prove your verbal aptitude by matching the entries in Column A with the appropriate words in Column B. It's OK to draw lines.

Column A	Column B
1. freedom	vibes
2. moral	party
3. participatory	backlash
4. pillbox	offensive
5. military-industrial	pig
6. flower	children
7. Day-Glo	band
8. guerrilla	fur
9. rat	decay
10. missile	kid stuff
11. Bass	art
12. pot	gap
13. white	theater
14. peace	bathing suit
15. Great	gap
16. talking	fink
17. nonverbal	joke
18. rice	communication
19. jug	Frontier
20. cultural	paint
21. generation	majority
22. pop	hat
23. computer	feeler
24. elephant	shop
25. topless	dating
26. Tet	blues
27. credibility	gap
28. fascist	Weejuns
29. mellow	democracy
30. fun	complex
31. New	Society
32. good	paddy
33. silent	revolution
34. head	ride
35. greasy	yellow

SCORE_____ × **10 points each** = _____ **(max. 350)**

● WHO THE HELL WAS FANNIE LOU HAMER?

10
Slogan Power!

It was the decade of the slogan and the chant. By this time you may not remember what they mean, but you should be able to finish them.

1. "Power to the _____."
2. "Off the _____."
3. "Do not fold, spindle, _____."
4. "Turn on, tune in, _____."
5. "Hell, no, _____."
6. "Dump _____."
7. "Make love, _____."
8. "In your heart, _____."
9. "Hey, hey, LBJ, _____."
10. "Ho, ho, Ho Chi Minh, _____."

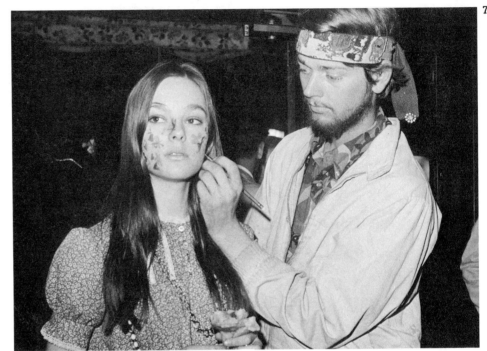

7

1

10

11. "The whole world is _____."
12. "Nixon's _____."
13. "Up against _____."
And speaking of slogans. . . .
14. "Free Huey!" refers to _____.
15. Rabelais said, *"Fay ce que voudras."* The hippies said, "Do your _____."

SCORE _____ × **10 points each =**
_____ **(max. 150)**

11
It Pays to Increase Your Word Power

1. Who introduced the word "super-califragilisticexpialidocious" to the world?

2. What, in California and the Southwest in the late Sixties, was *la causa?*

3. They called it "commercial bribery" and arrested Alan Freed for it. What was the more popular word for it in 1960? (Six letters.)

4. What kind of conclusion to the Vietnam War did Richard Nixon promise? (Nine letters.)

5. Chief nickname for LSD. (Four letters.)

6. Politically motivated destruction of property. (Eight letters.)

7. A semiorganized event during which people just hang around doing what they like. (Four letters, hyphenated.)

8. Publishing industry term for a work that doesn't have much content. (Seven letters.)

9. Tom Wolfe phrase to describe Leonard Bernstein's hosting a fundraiser for the Black Panther Party. (Two words.)

10. This phrase became a hotly debated topic in a presidential election. One side said, "We need it." The other side said, "It's code for repression." Remember?

SCORE_____ × **10 points each** =

_____**(max. 100)**

4

12
Compare and Contrast

What's the difference between

1. ... Marguerite Oswald and Marina Oswald?

2. ... Saul Alinsky and Adam Walinsky?

3. ... Grayson Kirk and Claude Kirk?

4. ... James Groppi and James Pike?

5. ... Robert Shelton and Robert Scheer?

6. ... George Whitmore and Richard Robles?

7. ... Robert Welch and Joseph Welch?

8. ... mods and rockers?

9. ... Sam Sheppard and Alan Shepard?

10. ... Agnon and Agnew?

SCORE_____ × **10 points each** =

_____**(max. 100)**

3a

3b

9a

9b

13
And One to Throw You for a Loop

This is Sandra Dee—Bobby Darin's wife, remember? Then there was Ruby Dee, the actress, and DeeDee Sharp, the singer. Now what about these "ee" types— all singers? Can you match them?

1. Joey Dee   sang "Sweet 16"

2. Bobby Vee   sang "Massachusetts"

3. The Bee Gees   sang "Devil or Angel"

4. B. B. King   sang "Peppermint Twist"

5. Dee Clark   sang "Raindrops"

SCORE_____ × 10 points each =

_____(max. 50)

● WHO THE HELL WAS JEAN SHRIMPTON?

14
High Fashion ... and Low

One, two, three, four—tell the people what we wore.

1. Who was credited (or blamed) with starting the miniskirt craze?

2. What designer made it big with topless bathing suits, although he first meant the whole thing as a joke?

3. What fun name was given to the totally topless swimsuit for women?

4. What kind of outfit did Allen Gins-berg wear in a popular 1960s poster?

5. Which movie did most to encourage the gangster look—striped double-breasted suits, superwide neckties, brown and white shoes?

6. And what did an Elizabeth Taylor movie do for the fashion world in 1962?

7. Who sent milliners rushing to produce enough pillbox hats to meet the demand?

8. Name two world leaders who had briefly popular jacket styles named for them.

9. When the Indian look came in among the young, beads were worn around the neck. What were they called?

10. Who designed Luci Johnson's bridal gown?

    A. Coco Chanel
    B. Mary Quant
    C. Priscilla of Boston
    D. Rheba of Highland Park
    E. Vivian Davis Polk

SCORE_____ × **10 points each** =

_____**(max. 100)**

10

16

15
Glorious Food

1. Terry Southern and Mason Hoffenburg's 1964 confection

2. In *The Ballad of John and Yoko,* what did J and Y eat in Vienna?

3. What world leader of the Sixties was once a cook under the great Escoffier?

4. In *Frankenstein Conquers the World,* a 1965 ripoff (one of many) of the Mary Shelley character, the monster eats

   A. beef Stroganoff
   B. sweetbreads
   C. cats and dogs
   D. liver
   E. anything with garlic

5. Not many dances have been named for foods. But DeeDee Sharp

5

sang about one. What was it? (Ten points extra credit for getting the exact title of the song as well as the dance.)

SCORE_____ × **10 points each** +

_____**extra** = _____**(max. 60)**

2

● WHO THE HELL WAS MANDY RICE-DAVIES?

16
Memorable Marriages

In the Sixties it became popular for couples to (gasp!) *live together.* Homosexuals (gasp!) began to come out of hiding. Divorce reached fad proportions, and communes were the rage. It looked as if marriage had had it. Still, some very important couples signed the papers. Remember?

1. Who raised eyebrows by marrying Happy Murphy?

2. Where were Herbert Khaury and Victoria May Budinger married on Dec. 17, 1969?

3. Whom did Patricia Boyd marry in 1966?

4. Where did Jackie marry Ari?

5. Where was Patrick Nugent's wedding reception?

6. One of the big marriages of the peace movement linked Joan Baez and _____.

7. Does the name Hope Cooke ring a bell? (Ten points extra credit for naming her alma mater.)

8. Thomas F. Manville married Christine Erdlen Papa on Jan. 11, 1960. So what?

9. Which celebrity couple staged a "bed-in" for peace during their honeymoon?

10. What rank was Charles Robb when he married Lynda Bird?

11. Ready? When Debbie and Eddie divorced so Eddie could marry Liz (whose third husband, Mike, had died in a plane crash), Debbie married _____. (Ten points extra credit: What was his business?)

18

12. Later, of course, after Liz and Eddie split and Liz married Dick, Eddie married _____.

13. Who was known in the press as the "runaway heiress," and what was the nationality of the man she loved? (Ten points extra credit: His name?)

14. It was an outdoor wedding. The bride wore a long gown and a crown of flowers. The groom wore bell bottoms. Judy Collins played and sang. His name was Arlo. What was hers?

15. Give the full name of the lucky lady who married Elvis Presley in Las Vegas on May 1, 1967.

SCORE_____ × 10 points each +

_____ extra = _____ (max. 180)

● WHO THE HELL WAS NORMAN F. DACEY?

17
Television

1. Andy Griffith was sheriff of _____.

2. On Oct. 1, 1962, the former host of *Who Do You Trust?* took over as host of another series. Who? What?

3. Of course, you know Fred Mac-Murray's brood on *My Three Sons*. But you need to know their dog's name. Was it

    A. Tramp?   **D.** Carlos?
    B. Bill?   **E.** Hund?
    C. Pushy?

4. What was the first live murder seen on television?

5. Sister Bertrille was known as the Flying Nun. This, however, is her colleague, Sister _____.▼

6. Who, in a highly rated Valentine's Day special in 1962, gave a tour of what building?

7. This is how they looked before their hair covered their ears. Now, aside from naming them, tell what instruments they played.

8. Who appeared with Howard K. Smith after Richard Nixon's "last press conference," to talk about the former veep?

● WHO THE HELL WAS EMILY HOFFERT?

9. Who tried her hand at a variety hour in place of the guys in question 7 after they were canceled?

10. What TV couple lived at 148 Bonnie Meadow Road, New Rochelle, N.Y.? (Hint: Alan Brady.)

11. One of TV's biggest contributions to monsterdom was *The Addams Family*. Name the family's butler, with the deep voice.

12. David Niven's 1964 series, with Charles Boyer, Gig Young, Robert Coote, and Gladys Cooper, was about a clan of con artists. Name it.

13. Whose voice spoke the lines of the title character in *My Mother the Car?* (Twenty points extra credit: What

make and year of car was the sweet lady?)

14. Remember *The Beverly Hillbillies?* Hard to forget Granny and the rest. What, then, was the Hillfolks' family name?

15. In 1960, CBS aired one of the sharpest and most controversial documentaries ever shown—about migrant farmworkers. Name it.

16. Whenever Henry Gibson read one of his poems, he began with the title, then said what?

17. Name the show that was boycotted by Italian-Americans in 1961.

18. In what prison camp were these men confined?▲

19. Speaking of military affairs, whose navy was this guy part of? And who was he?▼

20. What was *The Ev and Charlie Show?*

21. "There's a traffic jam in Harlem that's backed up to Jackson Heights." On what series?

22. Where did secret agent Maxwell Smart hide his telephone?

    A. His desk
    B. His shirt pocket
    C. His attaché case
    D. His shoe
    E. His wife

23. James Franciscus played Mr. Novak, the English teacher, in the TV series. But who was this man? (Ten points extra credit: Name their high school.)▼

24. Doc Severinsen was preceded by whom?

25

25. Name all four of these singing lads from television land. (Ten points extra
◄ credit: Name all their movies.)

SCORE_____ × **10 points each** +

_____ **extra** = _____ (max. 290)

23

22

22

Philosophy and Faith

1. What mass magazine gave cover treatment to a story analyzing the then current theological concern that "God is dead"?

2. The Beatles' favorite guru was _____?

3. Who was the American Marxist professor, author of *One-Dimensional Man,* who became the darling of student radicals?

4. What President's daughter converted to what religion on her 18th birthday?

5. Where have all the flowers gone?

6. Was Fidel Castro excommunicated?

7. In 1967 a college president asked to be relieved of religious vows and also requested that the college be secularized. The Roman Catholic Church said yes for the first time, to whom? (Ten points extra credit: What was the college?)

8. Who upset more than a few in the Roman Catholic Church when he

came out with such irreverencies as

> *Take whatever steps you want if*
> *You have cleared them with the*
> *pontiff*
>   *and*
> *Two, four, six, eight—*
> *Time to transsubstantiate!*

9. What sports arena in New York did a pope visit?

10. In 1964 two world figures met and exchanged "the kiss for peace." Who were they and what was it all about?

SCORE_____ × **10 points each** +

_____**extra** = _____**(max. 110)**

● WHO THE HELL WAS DR. CARL COPPOLINO?

19
If You Can't Answer This One, the Whole Decade Was a Waste

What's the proper response to "Say good night, Dick"?

SCORE_____ × 10 points = _____

(max. 10)

20
Alphabet

Sometimes even single letters have meaning. Identify and match:

1. J   Boss of Agent 007
2. M   Heroine, of sorts, of a Pauline Reage novel
3. O   Costa-Gavras movie of political turmoil
4. V   Author of *The Sensuous Woman*
5. Z   Novel by Thomas Pynchon

SCORE_____ × **10 points each** = _____ **(max. 50)**

21
A/K/A

Who were stuck with these nick-names?

1. Yaz
2. The Fab Four
3. Clean Gene
4. The Stilt
5. The Big Dipper
6. Westy
7. The Louisville Lip
8. Trane
9. *Der Alte*
10. Tricky Dick

SCORE_____ × **10 points each** =

_____ **(max. 100)**

● WHO THE HELL WAS RONALD L. RIDENHOUR?

The Movies

1. What boffo Sixties film begins with an aerial shot of mountains, then zooms down to a woman, arms outstretched, singing?

2. What was Barbra Streisand's first movie?

3. *Lover Come Back* was a 1961 picture starring the *Pillow Talk* pair. Who are they?

4. *Reptilicus,* a giant, toothy monster with an unsociable manner, wreaked havoc on what European city?
   - **A.** London
   - **B.** Stockholm
   - **C.** Copenhagen
   - **D.** Berlin
   - **E.** Bucharest

5. Charles Laughton and Clark Gable did it in 1935. Who did it in 1962? Did what?

6. What were the categories in the original 1968 Motion Picture Association of America classification system?

7. One of the talked-about imports of the decade contained a parenthetical color in the title. What was it?

8. Andy Warhol's first motion picture was eight hours long. It showed a man doing one thing for all eight hours. Doing what?

9. What did Pierre Boulle do?

10. You know Dennis Hopper costarred with Peter Fonda in *Easy Rider.* Did he also
    - **A.** write the film?
    - **B.** produce it?
    - **C.** direct it?
    - **D.** all of the above?

11. Mickey Spillane created detective Mike Hammer. Who played the Hammer role in the 1964 film *The Girl Hunters?*

12. Paul Newman was in five H movies of the Sixties. Two of them were *Harper and Hud.* Can you name the other three?

13. What was the 1963 comedy spectacular that featured dozens of well-known actors—from Milton Berle to Mickey Rooney to Sid Caesar to Jonathan Winters?

13

18

17

14. Match the movie monster with the description. You need all five for your ten points.

Ghidra	fanged flying fox
Dogora	toothed turtle
Gamera	three-headed
Ebirah	giant jellyfish
Gyaos	colossal crab

15. Who played Lolita?

16. Name a Leon Uris bestseller brought to the screen, complete with hit soundtrack. And name the producer.

17. Yes, Peter Sellers played the strange president in *Dr. Strangelove.* But what was the character's strange name? (Ten points extra credit: Give the film's subtitle.)

18. The motion picture *2001* also had a subtitle, which was _____?

21

19. A 1969 movie paired Elvis Presley with a nun in *Change of Habit*. Who played the nun?

20. Julie Christie won an Oscar for her portrayal of an amoral fashion model in what quintessential Sixties film?

21. Match the James Bond movie with the perils faced. Two points for each correct match (score separately).

A. *Thunderball*

B. *From Russia with Love*

C. *Goldfinger*

D. *You Only Live Twice*

E. *Dr. No*

F. nearly cut in two by a laser beam, almost decapitated by metal-brimmed derby

G. accosted by kidnappers at airport, surprised by tarantula in bed

H. crashed in plane, sealed in cave, smashed in hydrofoil, chased on motorcycle with flame thrower

I. chased by helicopter, menaced by Turkish wrestler, almost stabbed with poisoned blades secreted in Lotte Lenya's shoes

J. battled four helicopters alone in autogiro, escaped being blown up on island, nearly fell into pond of piranhas

22. The movie was *The Magnificent Seven*. Yul Brynner and Steve McQueen were the two best-known members of the group. For two points each, name the other five (score separately).

23. Here, alphabetically, are the Best Picture winners of the decade. Put them in chronological order, beginning with 1960. One point each (score separately).

A. *The Apartment*

B. *In the Heat of the Night*

C. *Lawrence of Arabia*

D. *A Man for All Seasons*

E. *Midnight Cowboy*

F. *My Fair Lady*

G. *Oliver!*

H. *The Sound of Music*

I. *Tom Jones*

J. *West Side Story*

24. What did Katharine Hepburn and Elizabeth Taylor each do twice in the Sixties? Details, please.

25. Which of these top-grossing films was *not* produced in the Sixties: *The Gradu-ate, Doctor Zhivago, Butch Cassidy and the Sundance Kid, The Ten Command-ments?*

26. What was the last line spoken in *Easy Rider?*

27. She played the lead in Myra Breckenridge, and for part of the time she—of all people—played a man. Who was she?

28. Name the movies that gave us these three theme songs: "Moon River" (1961), "The Shadow of Your Smile" (1965), and "Raindrops Keep Falling on My Head" (1969).

29. It was the story of an ex-soldier and five nuns. What actor won an Academy Award for it? And what was the film?

30. In the 1960's only one film won *four* of the top six Oscars (Best Picture, Actor, Actress, Supporting Actor, Supporting Actress, Director). Name the film and the award winners.

SCORE_____ × **10 points each** + _____**for partial answers (Nos. 21–23)** +

_____**extra** = _____**(max. 310)**

● WHO THE HELL WAS ARNOLD ZENKER?

23
Super Bonus Question in Arithmetic Agility

Take the number of Kennedy-Nixon debates. Add the number assigned to the Apollo shot that took Armstrong and Aldrin to the moon. Multiply by the number of seconds before the tapes self-destructed on *Mission: Impossible*. Subtract the favorite route number of Martin Milner, George Maharis, and their white convertible. Subtract a Fellini film. Result?

Score 50 points—all or nothing:

_____(max. 50)

24
The Story of Spiro

Fill in the blanks and read a fun story.

This is the story of Spiro _____ (1) Agnew. When first he burst upon our scene, even he admitted his name was "_____ _____ _____ _____ _____" (2). But before long Spiro was calling Vietnam Moratorium leaders an "_____ (3) corps of _____ _____" (4). Then he began talking about "the importance of the television news medium to the American people." The news is delivered by an "_____" (5) with "vast power," he said in a speech at a regional party meeting in _____ _____ (6). He also said of slums: "_____ _____ _____ _____, _____ _____ _____ _____" (7). And he started calling people insulting names like "_____" (8) and "_____ _____," (9) and he said Hubert Humphrey was "_____ _____ (10) on Communism." (Later he took that one back.) Then everyone admitted that his name *was* "_____ _____ _____" (see 2), and he lived happily ever after. Sort of.

SCORE_____ × 10 points each =

_____(max. 100)

● WHO THE HELL WAS CHARLOTTE MOORMAN?

25
Music: Take 25

1. Of whom did this group sing, "You were my first love, and you'll be my last love"? And name the group.

2. What Sixties group proclaimed that "Midwest farmers' daughters really make you feel all right"?

3. Who sang, "All the leaves are brown, and the sky is gray"?

4. A music superstar almost died in a motorcycle crash in 1966. Who?

5. Wrote "By the Time I Get to Phoenix" and "MacArthur Park" and "Up, Up, and Away": _____.

6. This guy was the type, according to one of his hits, "who likes to roam around." Can you name him, his group, *and* the hit?

7. A rare event: a "classical" album among the bestsellers. It was a Moog synthesizer recording of Bach. What was its title? (Ten points extra credit if you recall the electronic music man who did the work.)

8. Match to make groups' names. (You need *all* correct to score.)

A. Sly and the	Heat
B. Big Brother and the	Invention
C. Canned	Revival
D. The Grateful	Playboys
E. Creedence Clearwater	Family Stone
F. Butterfield	Who
G. The Lovin'	Holding Company
H. The	Dead
I. The Mothers of	Spoonful
J. Gary Lewis and the	Blues Band

9. What can stop the Duke of Earl?

10. The year 1963 was big for rumors. There was this song by the Kingsmen, see, and you couldn't really understand the words but everyone just *knew* they were really raunchy, and if you could just slow down the record a little and listen real carefully you could maybe hear something awful. . . . What was the song?

11. And what was the most widespread rumor about Paul McCartney?

1

6

11

12. This is the Drifters, who sang, "Don't forget who's takin' you home, and in whose arms you're gonna be." Considering that situation, what command did they give? ▼

12

24

13. Fillmore East and Fillmore West were legendary music halls run by _____?

14. In 1962 _____ succeeded _____ as music director of the Boston Symphony.

15. What jazz musician was honored with a 70th birthday party at the White House?

16. And what classical composer was so honored by President Kennedy on his 80th?

17. What did Aretha Franklin do to the Beatles' "Eleanor Rigby"?

18. Who was the guy Johnny Cash sang about in "The Ballad of Ira Hayes"?

19. Whom did Running Bear love?

20. What cellist performed solo at the Kennedy White House?

21. What's the style of music that combined the Brazilian samba with modern American jazz?

22. And what was that music's first big hit song, first recorded by Stan Getz and Charlie Byrd?

23. Who started the Twist?

24. "Raga rock" was a hybrid music played on the _____, popularized by _____, who was taught by _____.

25. According to Malvina Reynolds, what were the little boxes on the hillside all made out of?

SCORE_____ × **10 points each** + _____**extra** = _____**(max. 260)**

● WHO THE HELL WAS RUDI DUTSCHKE?

26
The Letter N

1. _ _ _ _ _ <u>N</u> (Where they put up a wall.)

2. _ _ _ _ _ _ <u>N</u> (Southwest Texas State Teachers College grad.)

3. _ _ _ _ _ _ _ <u>N</u> (Presidential nomination seeker from Pennsylvania)

4. _ _ _ _ _ <u>N</u> (Screamer with Big Brother and pals.)

5. _ _ _ _ <u>N</u> (Né Zimmerman.)

SCORE_____ × **10 points each =**

_____ **(max. 50)**

27
Complete the Quote

1. "Michael, row the boat ashore, _____."

2. "Hare krishna, hare krishna, _____ _."

3. "War is not healthy for _____."

4. "Come now, and let us _____."

5. "I have a _____."

6. "We stand today on the edge of _____."

7. "I can't get no _____."

8. "All the lonely people, _____."

9. "Sock it _____."

10. "Sorry about that, _____."

SCORE_____ × **10 points each =**

_____ **(max. 100)**

28
Campaign Stuff

Name the chief losing teams in the presidential elections of the Sixties. (Ten points extra credit for supplying five of the six middle names; another ten for the sixth.)

1. 1960: _____ _____ _____ and _____ _____ _____

2. 1964: _____ _____ _____ and _____ _____ _____

3. 1968: _____ _____ _____ and _____ _____ _____

4. Who was George Wallace's running mate in 1968? (Ten points extra credit: What was his previous job?)

5. Who was Richard Nixon's strongest challenger in the 1960 Republican nomination fight?

6. Negative points were given Nixon during the debate with Kennedy for his lack of knowledge about which two islands?

7. LBJ and HHH were nominated by acclamation at the '64 Democratic National Convention. In what coastal city?

   A. San Francisco
   B. Atlantic City
   C. Boston
   D. Miami
   E. San Diego

8. Eugene McCarthy was given reason to hope when he won more than _____ percent of the vote in the New Hampshire primary.

   A. 32   **D.** 62
   B. 42   **E.** 72
   C. 52

7

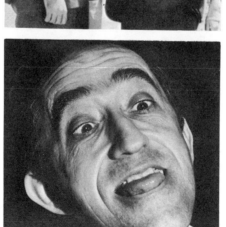

9

10. In 1968 the Democratic convention in Chicago was the memorable one, full of blood, sweat, and tear gas. In our minds it has cleanly upstaged that year's Republican confab, in which the Nixon-Agnew team was molded. How many ballots were taken before Nixon won?

SCORE_____ × 10 points each +

_____ extra = _____ (max. 130)

9. What TV comic, with first and last initials the same, ran for President in 1968?

29
True or False?

1. Frank Borman walked on the moon.

2. Ebbets Field was converted to an indoor athletic facility.

3. Nikita Khrushchev was once a coal miner.

4. Princeton gave Bob Dylan an honorary degree.

5. Despite a string of pitching accomplishments, Tom Seaver didn't win the Cy Young Award until the 1970s.

6. Mayor Daley testified at the trial of the Chicago Seven.

7. Glen Campbell was once a Beach Boy.

8. Milton Berle hosted *Bowling for Dollars* on television.

9. Jack Ruby never wore hats.

10. The Beatles were made members of the Order of the British Empire.

11. Bishop Pike questioned many orthodox theological notions, but there were two pieces of doctrine he said must be accepted by all Christians: the divinity of Jesus and the Trinity.

12. The U.S.A. offered Cuba storm-relief aid in 1963 but was rejected.

13. The beer-can tab opener first became big in the Sixties.

14. A special law was enacted in Israel to allow the execution of Lieutenant Colonel Adolf Eichmann.

15. Spiro Agnew nominated Richard Nixon in 1968.

SCORE_____ × 10 points each = _____ (max. 150)

30
In the Middle

Start by supplying the middle initials for these five names from the Sixties:

1. Julius _____ Hoffman
2. Lewis _____ Hershey
3. Nicholas _____ Katzenbach
4. Captain James _____ Kirk
5. Christiaan _____ Barnard

On the next five, give complete middle names. Nothing easy like Fitzgerald and Milhous. A little harder:

6. Billie _____ Estes
7. Robert _____ McNamara

8. Jorge _____ Borges
9. Nikita _____ Khrushchev
10. Cassius _____ Clay

SCORE _____ × **10 points each** =

_____ **(max. 100)**

● WHO THE HELL WAS JACK RUBENSTEIN?

31
Rivers and Islands

1

1. Where was Chairman Mao reported to have swum nine brisk miles at age 72?

2. Who was the Sixties' best-known lover of the island of Bimini?

3. What river overflowed its banks in 1966, damaging large parts of an important art city?

4. Ted Kennedy said he and Mary Jo Kopechne were headed for a ferry from Chappaquiddick island back to where?

5. Christmas Island is best known as
  A. summit meeting site
  B. presidential retreat
  C. nuclear test site
  D. fashion center
  E. toy market

SCORE_____ × **10 points each =**

_____**(max. 50)**

1. The controversial play about Pope Pius XII in wartime was called *The Deputy*. It made its German playwright famous in short order. Is his name still with you?

2. What was the name of Gore Vidal's play about a fight for the presidential nomination?

3. Remember *Bye-Bye Birdie?* Why did Birdie go bye-bye?

4. Lillian Hellman play: _____ *in the* _____.

5. They sat on a stage, just the two of them, and made an audience laugh all evening. They hit with a big show that opened in 1960 with an eight-word title and a lot of good material. Name that big show, and you'll name them too.

6. Can you give the complete 26-word title of the Peter Weiss play popularly known as *Marat/Sade?*

7. Speaking of long titles, complete this one: *Oh Dad, Poor Dad, _____.* (Ten points extra credit: Who wrote it?)

8. Name the satirical play about a politician who, urged by his wife, sets up the assassination of President John Ken O'Dunc. (Ten points extra credit: Name the author.)

9. Who was Claude Hooper Bukowski?

10. Which show featured a smash song that spoke of "the unbeatable foe"?

SCORE _____ × 10 points each +

_____ extra = _____ (max. 120)

5

33
Vowel Play

Below, accompanied by clues, are some Sixties names that end in a vowel. The vowels are gifts. You fill in the rest.

1. _ _ _ _ _ _ _ _ _ A
(Mother of Invention.)

2. _ _ _ _ _ A v. _ _ _
_ _ A (1966 Supreme Court decision on defendant rights; two names, still only ten points.)

3. _ _ _ _ _ _ _ _ _ _ _ E
(Resigned as President.)

4. _ _ _ E (Resigned as *le Président.*)

5. _ _ _ _ _ _ _ _ _ O
(Disgraced British War Secretary.)

SCORE_____ × **10 points each** =

_____**(max. 50)**

34
ID, Please

These five characters are all products of someone's imagination. Identify.

1. Little Jackie Paper
2. Percy Dovetonsils
3. Mr. Kite
4. Frodo Baggins
5. Norman Bates

SCORE_____ × **10 points each** =

_____**(max. 50)**

● WHO THE HELL WAS VALENTINA TERESHKOVA?

35
Sports

1. What year was the first Super Bowl? Who won?

2. OK—who *lost?* And what was the score?

3. Jackie Gleason played the role of a pool sharpie in a 1961 movie; name the sharpie and name the picture.

4. Through the decade, until the amazing year of 1969, the Mets were out of the National League cellar only twice, each time to ninth place. Which years?

5. Who was the former welterweight champ who died after being knocked out by Emile Griffith in a 1962 fight?

6. What did Frank Robinson and Carl Yastrzemski both do in the Sixties?

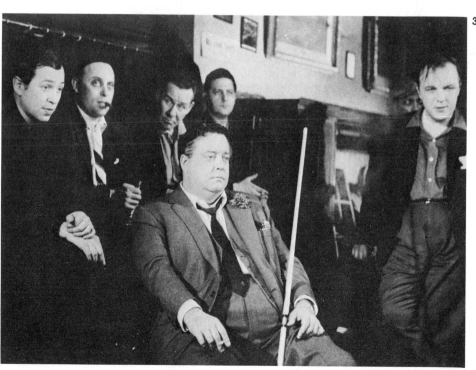

3

7. In 1960, Floyd Patterson became the first ex-heavyweight champ to win back his title, knocking out _____.

8. This Australian starred in the 1960 Olympics at Rome, running 1,500 meters in 3:35.6. Name him.

9. What was Kareem Abdul-Jabbar's original name? Spelling counts.

10. What game did Nikita Khrushchev and Dean Rusk play? Who won?

11. Who won the Indy 500 three times in the Sixties?

12. With what two pro teams did George Plimpton practice quarterbacking?

13. How many times did Casey Stengel retire in the Sixties?

14. Who first threw the 16-pound steel shotput more than 70 feet?

15. In 1966 the Yankees did something that amazed everyone. They hadn't done it in 55 years. What?

16. Who was Kauai King?

17. Using a newly improved fiberglass pole, John Pennel was the first person to pole vault 17 feet. By how much did he exceed that mark in that first record-breaking jump?

18. Match the football star with the college he attended. (You need all four right answers for your ten points.)

Roger Staubach	USC
Mike Garrett	Syracuse
O. J. Simpson	Navy
Ernie Davis	USC

19. Who hurled 58 consecutive shutout innings for the Dodgers in 1968?

20. What did Rod Laver do that hadn't been done since Don Budge did it 25 years earlier?

21. Who, in 1963, established a record for golf earnings but didn't win a single national championship?

22. What happened to Wilt Chamberlain on Mar. 2, 1962?

23. He came from Abruzzi, Italy, and won the World Wide Wrestling Federation's championship belt and kept it a long time. His name was _____?

24. Who was the only player ever to pinch-hit for Ted Williams?

25. On Nov. 17, 1968, the last two minutes of the telecast of the Jets-Raiders game were preempted by a network movie, with the score Jets 32, Raiders 29. During those two minutes Oakland scored twice, winning 43–32 and infuriating millions. What movie was shown?

SCORE _____ × **10 points each** = _____ (max. 250)

36
Ha-Ha-Ha

1. What's huge and purple and swims in the ocean?

2. What's purple and hums?

3. Why does it hum?

4. How can you tell if an elephant has been in your refrigerator?

5. "Ho-hum, the train's derailed," said Tom distractedly. What's that an example of?

SCORE_____ × **10 points each =**

_____**(max. 50)**

47

37
The Number Game

1. How many minutes a day does the Royal Canadian Air Force exercise plan require of men? Of women?

2. Officially, how many stars were on the U.S. flag on Jan. 1, 1960?

3. According to the title of her memoirs, Svetlana Alliluyeva wrote _____ *Letters to a Friend*

4. On TV's *Get Smart*, Don Adams and Barbara Feldon played agents with which of these numbers?

 A. 86 **D.** 000
 B. 96 **E.** 30
 C. 99

5. What uniform number did the Red Sox retire in 1960? Why? (Ten points extra credit: What happened just before the suit was hung up?)

6. The Soviet spaceships that first docked in space, allowing cosmonauts to move from one craft to the other, were Soyuz ships number _____ and _____.

7. A 1968 François Truffaut movie: *Fahrenheit _____.*

8. On *Star Trek* how many years was the *Enterprise*'s mission to be?

9. How old did Mel Brooks tell Carl Reiner he was in 1961?

10. In January 1963 the price of a first-class letter went from _____ cents to _____ cents. In 1968 it went to _____ cents.

11. In 1960, when McDonald's was just beginning to take over America, how many hamburgers did their signs

say had been sold? What did the signs say at the close of the decade in 1969?

12. The number of Jack Kennedy's PT boat?

13. TV's *The Munsters* lived on Mockingbird Lane. What number?

14. How many men died in the battle between Snoopy and the Red Baron?

15. How many orbits of the earth did John Glenn make in that first important shot?

SCORE _____ × **10 points each** +

● WHO THE HELL WAS LOUIS WOLFSON?

38
Isn't That Whatsisname?

1. Abrasive talk-show host. Not a smash.▼

2. Congolese general, fond of coups.▲

3. Once sang of his "sweet fräulein down in Berlin town" and his "China doll in old Hong Kong."▶

4. Ed Sullivan's bookends were a Canadian comedy team. (Ten points extra credit for knowing both first names.)▲

5. SDS chief usually seen without beard. ▲

SCORE_____× **10 points each** +

_____ **extra** = _____(**max. 60**)

39
Who Died?

1. Oft-busted comic, 1966.
2. Vaudevillian, radio star, TV star, once lost her brother, 1964.

3. Sang about chestnuts roasting, 1965.

4. Animator supreme, 1966.

5. Old pardner, had horse named Calico and mule named Blossom, 1969.

6. Married to Kay Williams Spreckels (No. 5) when he died, 1960.

7. William Henry Pratt, 1969.

17. Angelo Giuseppe Roncalli, 1963.

18–20. Three astronauts, in a simulated rocket launch, 1967.

SCORE_____ × **10 points each =**

_____ **(max. 200)**

8. Oliver's partner, 1965.

9. The Grand Old Man of Football, 1965.

10. Last of the Red Hots, 1966.

11. Noted party giver E. M., 1963.

12. Infant son of John and Jacqueline Kennedy, 1963.

13. Lyricist for *South Pacific, The King and I,* and *Oklahoma!,* 1960.

14. Honked a horn and played a harp, real name Arthur, 1964.

15. Manners maker, 1960.

16. Three-initialed wit of Round Table and *Information Please,* 1960.

● WHO THE HELL WAS DONALD SLAYTON?

How Did They Die?

Five more Sixties deaths of note. This time, play medical examiner and choose the cause of death from the column at right.

1. Ernest Hemingway, 1961
2. Ernie Kovacs, 1962
3. Marilyn Monroe, 1962
4. Thomas Merton, 1968
5. Rocky Marciano, 1969

Auto crash

Freak electrocution in a train

Plane crash

Overdose of pills

Self-inflicted gunshot wound

SCORE _____ × **10 points**

each = _____ **(max. 50)**

1

3

41

Forgery Identification

Can you tell which is the real signature?

A.

B.

C.

D.

E.

Score 20 points for right answer =

______(max. 20)

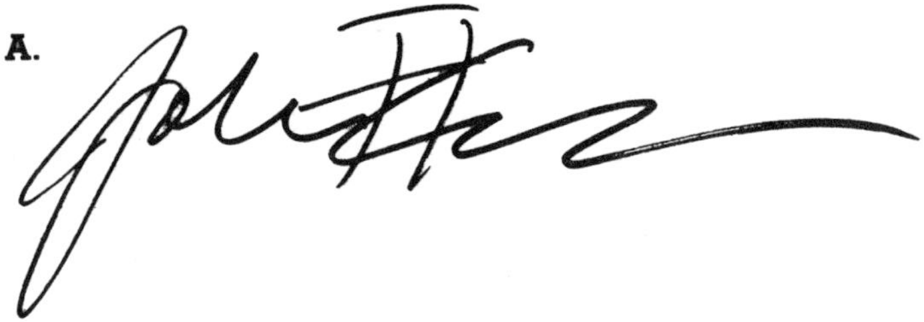

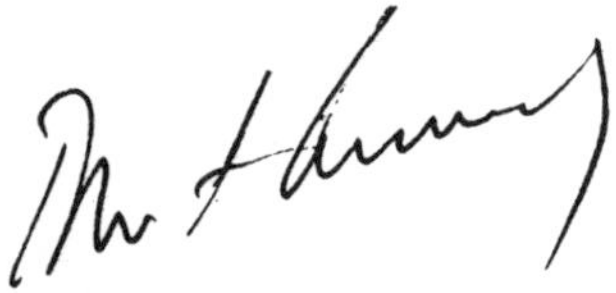

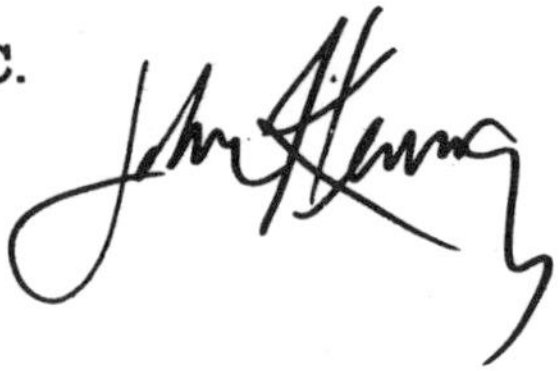

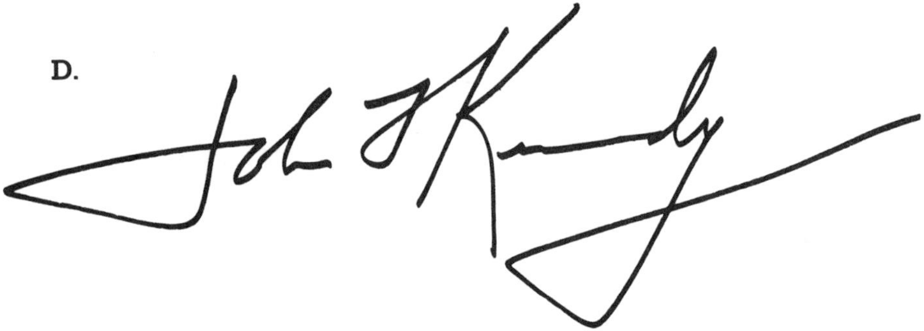

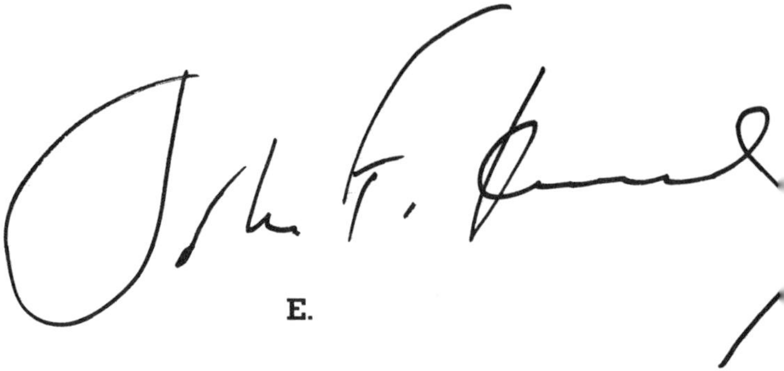

42
Books

1. What funny book contains the line, "Who promoted Major Major?"

2. What was the best-selling red-plastic-covered book of the decade?

3. Repeat the Peter Principle precisely, please.

4. Who wrote a witty, name-dropping anecdotal autobiography called *The Memoirs of an Amnesiac?*

5. And who called his life story *How to Talk Dirty and Influence People?*

6. And whose posthumous autobiography, *My Wicked, Wicked Ways,* was a big seller in 1960?

7. How about *Yes I Can?* Whose life was that?

8. Tom Wolfe's 1965 smasher. (Seven words in the title; spelling counts.)

9. It was a heavy book. They called it the third. Some critics said the second was better. What was it?

10. Who were Cooper's Poopers?

11. Who was the only American to win the Nobel Prize for Literature in the Sixties?

12. What was *Mandate for Change* all about?

13. A young lawyer wrote this one, and it triggered federal legislation. Figure it out: U_____ a_____ A_____ S_____, by R_____ N_____.

14. Who admonished: "You heard your mother. Don't eat French fries with Melvin Weiner after school . . . or ever."

15. What was noteworthy about *Report from Iron Mountain?* (Ten points extra credit: Who wrote it?)

16. The controversial book was published in Paris in 1934, but its American author had to wait until 1961 to see it released in his own country because he had been loose with his language. The book was hailed as a masterpiece, and the author did a sequel with a title the same except for the final word. Tell all.

17. "She'd take two of them tonight. Why not? After all, it was New Year's Eve!" That's the end of what torrid big novel?

18. "While it is true that the book is well-written, such fact does not condone its indecency." Written by a three-judge court in Manhattan, 1963. The "obscene" book: *Memoirs of a Woman of Pleasure,* better known as _____?

19. Who rode with the Hell's Angels to gather material for a book? What happened to him?

20. What was the name of Piri Thomas'

bestseller, and to what ethnic group did Thomas belong?

21. Who put captions to news photos for the best-selling novelty book *Who's in Charge Here?*

22. One of the most talked-about books of the decade began with this sentence, which includes what became one of the most quoted statements of the times: "In a culture like ours, long accustomed to splitting and dividing all things as a means of control, it is sometimes a bit of a shock to be reminded that, in operational and practical fact, _____ _____ _____ _____ _____." Fill in the five blanks. (Ten points extra credit: Give the author *and* title.)

23. Franny and Zooey's last name, please.

24. In New York, U.S. Circuit Court of Appeals Chief Judge Charles E. Clark ruled a celebrated book not obscene: "Should a mature and sophisticated reading public be kept in blinders because a government official thinks reading certain works of power and literary value are not good for him?" What government official? What book?

25. Who, in what book, asked, for American women, "Is this all?"

SCORE_____ × 10 **points each** + _____ **extra** = _____ (max. 270)

55

43
Initials

Just tell what they mean, please, PDQ.

1. NLF
2. SNCC
3. SDS
4. MIRV
5. ROTC
6. CO
7. VC
8. DMZ
9. TWTWTW (or TW3)
10. SPECTRE
11. CORE
12. YAF
13. YIP
14. VISTA
15. LNS
16. LEM
17. UNCLE
18. THRUSH
19. WRL
20. FSM

SCORE_____ × **10 points each** =

_____**(max. 200)**

44
Giant Sixties Word Find

Word find puzzles are a phenomenon of the Seventies, but here's one based on names, words, and phrases that speak of the Sixties. A sharp and persistent pair of eyes can ferret out 66 of them, deftly buried in the letter grid. They fit in here, there, and around: left to right, right to left, top to bottom, bottom to top, diagonally both ways.

We gave you two points for nothing. Score one point for each find up to 50 counting the freebees, two points for each through 60, three points for the next five, and a rewarding 15 points if you find No. 66. That totals 100 points. Good luck.

SCORE 1 × _____ **for 1–50** = _____,

2 × _____ **for 51–60** = _____, **3** ×

_____ **for 61–65** = _____, **15 for 66**

= _____; **total:** _____ **(max. 100)**

```
L L E D U C T H O J R D A Y S O F R A G E S L E R T S N I M Y T S I R H C W E N
F O V I Z E R R T U O P S Y C H E D E L I C L A N N O D E N A C I R R U H H Q C
R T E S L E R D G D M S A R D O M M U O Y E H A L I C A N D L O U D Q M M U Z O
U U R C O D E D R Y H M C R A S Z Y L D A V I D B E N G U R I O N S O R T N V O
G N G O A J P O E C N O D N O B N A I L U J N J K A L M D O N K N O T T S L I L
M A R K R U D D E O T T N P R S C L B I A A K I O N Q B E L M O N D O L R I E H
S B E I N H A M N L T H T K A M D A C E M I C K E Y H A R G I T A Y Y D W A T A
A U E K Z A H C B L T E E A Y D R I E D I G A S T R O N A U T Z Z F R D O R N N
R R N O A L K C E I D R I R L Y A B O A L A M P Y B T P N D I D O Y O A R T A D
Z N R P L M S I R N A S H I E E H O A N O Y R Y B G Y N R F L B F D G L K H M L
N B E I R I S F E S L B Y N W A G R A B M O A N S E L W O B R E T S E H C N I U
O A V W N U B S T C I R H C T L L J D G I F N A J G E L V S T D S E R H E I Z K
O B I S T T F S A N G O N E U Q O I W E N R H S E L M A T Y U M I H G N I M A E
P Y E A N N O Y N N A T S A D B R F S G D H B C B S W D N U O U D Y K M N I T C
O B W B A F E A U H L H P T W L I L C T E T A Y R A Y R E N H S T I C O A H I R
E U S A K O C H R O S E E A I A A L Y O R A Y A R B I I R D Y K A A I R L C O E
E R L S T T E S R E I R Y O T C S D A P B O L H E L L B G E T I L V D I V O N H
A N N O A H R N O U C S T O F K T S E R I T R F V I S A T R E E B I N M M H A C
N K O T T C T J Y A A A O A W I E M G O N N A P A L M D E G B R T I A A L X F A
D A S I X D A Y W A R C N H T S I O L S D I I A E E G N I R F E H T D N O Y E B
R H N M A O M M R K L T P H Q B N T L E E K C N L A R Y M O N T E R F O L D T L
E L A I S I N N A F O I L N B E E T L Y R N T T C S A L P U B C A O E F D R F E
A I M N D U B A G M G Y A A I A M O A G T O H Y E C C E R N W D N D L L T S S H
L L S O F Y V I K B L H C T H U A B W R N T Y H G H E L T D T R I V I A E T F C
A G E S G T C R K N E M E C T T R L N I E F S O D P S W A P T I M M I M D I B S
C I L F H R M A N K S D D A D I E L I E L O T S I I L D L R T S A E B A O L B A
K B R E N E O S F H B P F T P F F E L R A F L E R A I G P E D K L O C N T L G A
L R A R J U L S N F Y E D N L U O B R I T L R G D N C D O S O F S T H C F M H Z
W A H F L Q J O Y M U P A R Y L A K E E S U R A L T K G O S B M A N T H U A E I
I N C H I T T Y C H I T T Y B A N G B A N G U Y E N C A O K Y S F O L A S N S L
```

45
What's My Line?

Your job is to tell just what their jobs were.

1. Lovely Rita
2. Veruschka
3. Dickens and Fenster
4. Clouseau

5

10

5. Ronald Reagan (immediately before he entered politics—be specific)
6. Obie
7. Oscar Madison
8. El Exigente
9. Hazel (Shirley Booth role)
10. Edward R. Murrow (after TV)
11. Yevgeny Yevtushenko
12. Che Guevara (pre-Revolution)
13. Philip Blaiberg (heart transplant survivor)
14. Bobby Baker
15. Toody and Muldoon

SCORE_____ × 10 points each = _____ (max. 150)

● WHO THE HELL WAS LORD HARLECH?

46
The Letter X

1. _ _ _ _ _ X (either/or clothing)

2. _ _ _ _ _ X (MVP southpaw)

3. _ _ _ _ _ _ _ X (versatile artist-designer)

4. _ _ X _ _ _ _ _ (the longest style outerwear)

5. _ _ _ _ _ _ _ _ _ X

_ X _ _ _ _ _ _ _ (acid rock group)

SCORE_____ × **10 points each =**

_____**(max. 50)**

47
Magazines

1. What happened to which major magazine in February 1969? (Hint: Norman Rockwell.)

2. What was "the magazine of sexual candor," published by Ralph Ginzburg, which raised eyebrows more for a sequence of biracial poses and some zippy ads than for the explicitness of its sexual photos?

3. Which magazine did Jackie Kennedy sue over planned publication of portions of *Death of a President?* (Ten points extra credit: Name the author.)

4. Which magazine did Wally Butts sue for libel over a football-fix story? (Ten points extra credit if you remember his job.)

5. Which magazine turned over a whole issue to Norman Mailer to write about the march on the Pentagon? (Ten points extra credit: The same month, another magazine devoted *its* entire issue to another single writer; details?)

SCORE_____ × **10 points each +**

_____**extra =**_____**(max. 80)**

● WHO THE HELL WAS ROSS BARNETT?

A Smattering of Crime

1. In 1966 eight student nurses were stabbed to death by one man. Give the name of the killer and the city.

2. Less than three weeks later another mass murderer struck—this time by spraying passersby with bullets from atop a tower. Where did this episode take place, and who was the man responsible?

3. What senator's 21-year-old daughter was murdered in bed?

4. About how much money was taken in the Great Train Robbery of Cheddington, England?

5. Name the gangster who yakked to a Senate subcommittee about organized crime in America.

6. What phrase did he use to de-

scribe the underworld's central organization?

7. The son of a superstar said he had been kidnapped. Not many believed him. Who was it?

8. What color hair did Alice Crimmins have?

9. The "Zodiac Killer" struck in what state?

10. Francis Gary Powers, the U-2 pilot shot down over Russia in 1960, was declared an American spy and sentenced to ten years in a Soviet prison. He was released, however, in 1962, in exchange for one of *their* convicted spies. Name the Russian.

SCORE_____ × **10 points each =**

_____**(max. 100)**

49
What's Happening?

1. Mama has just lost. Who's Mama, and what has she lost?▲

2. Judging from what you see here, ◄ what holiday is approaching?

3. What is the bald fellow demonstrating to the fellow with the sideburns?▲

4. Who is this man, and what is he holding?▼

5. It's a burning issue these two are discussing. Can you tell? ▼

6. Who's the hot dancer? (He was an LBJ aide)▲

7. This Kansan is about to break the tape. Does it matter?▼

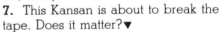

9. The man on the left looks serious; the man on the right looks even seriouser. Why?▲

8. Who are these lovelies and what ◀ are they doing?

10. Why is this man happy?▲

SCORE_____ × **10 points each =**

_____**(max. 100)**

About Women

1. GOVERNOR'S MOM BUSTED Explain. ▶

2. Where did she go to college? ▼

3. What did she say her job was?▲

◀**4.** Which of the following Dylan songs did this woman record?

    A. "Tomorrow Is a Long Time"
    B. "Mr. Tambourine Man"
    C. "Daddy, You've Been on My Mind"
    D. "Farewell"

5. Who was her boyfriend? (Character name and the actor, please.)▲

SCORE_____ × **10 points each =**
_____**(max. 50)**

●WHO THE HELL WAS ALBERT DESALVO?

51
Hidden Words

Imbedded in these strange sentences are important words of the Sixties. Ignore spacing, punctuation, and meaning. Find the words.

Example: THE 'GAME OF RUG-BY' IS NO GAME—IT'S WARFARE. (Dance)

1. I NEARLY WORSHIP PIES MADE WITH TART APPLES. (Category of citizen.)

2. A MORATORIUM IS AN ANTI-WAR HOLIDAY, ISN'T IT? (Artist.)

3. IT TAKES TWO TO CHANGE A LIGHT BULB? JERK! (Pres.)

4. A BANANA PALM? MUST BE THE FRUIT OF YOUR IMAGINATION. (Weapon.)

5. THEY MET AT A COLUMBIA FRAT PARTY, WHERE GOOD ROCK WAS PLAYED. (Struggling nation.)

6. THAT MAN'S ON MY "BAD GUY" LIST . . . AND EVERYBODY ELSE'S. (Head of family.)

7. GIVE THE FLY A SWAT, TSAR NICHOLAS! (Los Angeles neighborhood.)

8. A LAUGH? AN "OI-OI-OI" WOULD BE MORE LIKE IT. (Oriental capital.)

9. MILTON . . . FUNNY MILTON . . . KIND MILTON . . . THEY CALLED HIM "MR. TELEVISION." (Early Viet trouble spot.)

10. WE SAY "OF COURSE" IN AMERICA. THEY SAY "NATÜRLICH" IN GERMANY. (Book that tells all.)

SCORE_____ × **10 points each =**

_____**(max. 100)**

● WHO THE HELL WAS SHORTY POWERS?

52
Friendly Animals

1. Name Caroline Kennedy's pony.

2. Walt Disney Studios did a movie in 1961 about more than 100 dogs of a certain breed. How many, precisely, and what breed?

3. Who created Fritz the Cat, of underground comix fame?

4. He was a Fifties dog, really, but he died in 1964, age 12, and was buried in the Bide-a-Wee Pet Memorial Park on Long Island, N.Y. Name him and give his breed.

5. What was the name of the pet pig on television's *Green Acres?*

6. Remember LBJ's beagles—the ones he hoisted up by the ears? Name them.

6

7. In John Steinbeck's *Travels with Charlie,* the Charlie in question is an animal. Just what type? (Ten points extra credit: Give Charlie's color and full name.)

8. The biggest song by an Australian in the Sixties was a ditty about—naturally—a kangaroo. The title?

9. Name TV's talking horse.

10. The first animal to orbit the earth under the U.S. flag (in 1961) was a chimp named _____?

11. A dolphin that kids loved on TV.

12. What pig was put up for the presidency in 1968?

13. What was the name of the elephant at the 1968 Republican National Convention?

14. Where's the best place to put a tiger?

15. What goes on, according to the song by the Tokens, "in the jungle, the quiet jungle?" (Hint: Wimoweh.)

SCORE_____ × **10 points each** +

_____ **extra** = _____ **(max. 160)**

1

11

53
Music: Take 20 More

1. The Singing Nun sang about a chap named _____.

2. Song opening: "She wore blue _____."

3. Getting together to sing and listen to folk songs wasn't called a songfest or a concert or a jam session. What was it called?

4. What dance did this little lady introduce?▲

5. Which rock singer flashed to the audience in March 1969? (Ten points extra credit: Where did it happen?)

6. What can't you get at Alice's Restaurant?

7. Which of these is *not* a Dylan album title?
   A. *Nashville Skyline*
   B. *The Freewheelin' Bob Dylan*
   C. *Self Portrait*
   D. *John Wesley Harding*
   E. *Dylan Goes Home*
   F. *Highway 61 Revisited*
   G. *Blonde on Blonde*

8. Who sang "Downtown"?

9. What camp did Allan Sherman sing about?

10. Who discovered the Beatles?

11. What, according to Gene McDaniels, was made from 100 pounds of clay?

12. The "Never on Sunday" theme was a smash. Who recorded it?

13. There aren't many songs that refer to girls by number instead of name. But there was at least one, and she sounds like a thermometer reading. Who was she?

14. What unorthodox jazzman graced the cover of *Time* magazine in the mid-Sixties, wearing a hat? (Ten points extra credit for spelling his name right.)

15. What group asked what girl, "Won't you come out tonight?" (Ten points extra credit if you can name each member.)

16. What wouldn't "the widder next door" have?

17. What duo sang "Soul and Inspiration" and "You've Lost That Lovin' Feelin'"? (Ten points extra credit for remembering both their names.)

18. Rock with a message. Best known for thumbing their noses (and making other gestures) at society, this group transformed Allen Ginsberg's "Howl" into a song they called "I Saw the Best Minds of My Generation Rock." Their leader was Ed Sanders. Name the group.

19

15

19. The man with the teeth was so taken with a girl he was "Tossin' and Turnin'" over her. Can you name him?▲

20. What group ended concerts by smashing instruments on stage?

SCORE_____ × **10 points each +**

_____**extra** = _____**(max. 240)**

● WHO THE HELL WAS JOSEPH GARGAN?

54
Colors

Can you match the colors on the right to the entries on the left?

1. P. Sellers film   blue

2. Pepperland's enemies   green

3. Itsy-bitsy teeny-weeny polka-dot bikini   pink

4. Jefferson Airplane's rabbit   yellow

5. Sperry & Hutchinson color   white

SCORE_____ × **10 points each** = _____**(max. 50)**

55
Strikes, Protests, Riots, Etc.

1. On Feb. 1, 1960, the first of a series of black sit-ins took place when

four North Carolina Agricultural and Technical College freshmen quietly refused to leave a lunch counter in Greensboro, N.C. What lunch counter? (Ten points extra credit: What did they try to order?)

2. The Free Speech Movement at Berkeley, the decade's first big student revolt, began over an administration decision

    A. to censor the school newspaper

    B. to censor the school literary magazine
    C. to restrict solicitation for off-campus political groups
    D. to ban comments from classroom floors
    E. to charge a registration fee to candidates for student council

3. What and when was the Port Huron Statement?

4. Who was Hugh Addonizio?

5. The famous Chicago Seven was first the Chicago Eight. What happened?

6. You knew this one was coming: Name the Chicago Seven. All of them. (Not to be confused with the Seven Dwarfs, who were never brought to trial.)

7. Whose birthday weren't the Seven allowed to celebrate in court with a cake? And which number birthday was it?

8. Two Florida cities figured heavily in Sixties news—one for attracting mobs of college students for raucous vacation blasts, one for racial turmoil when segregated-beach rules were put to the test. Name the cities.

9. Give the full name of the French student strike leader known as Danny the Red.

10. What group took over a famous island in 1969, claiming it belonged to them? (Ten points extra credit: What holiday did they celebrate during the occupation?)

SCORE_____ × **10 points each** +

_____**extra** = _____**(max. 120)**

Words from Our Sponsors

1. What product was said to be good if you wanted to "take it off—take it *all* off"?

2. What product claimed it could help shave sandpaper?

3. Complete: "Cleans like a White _____!" (And name the product.)

4. Who's come a long way?

5. Among the various rebellions of the Sixties was one cooked up by Detroit and Madison Avenue, the aim of which was to sell cars. What was this rebellion called?

6. What kind of headaches are numbered?

7. "Mother, *please*—I'd rather _____ _____ _____!" (And name the product.)

8. "That li'l old _____—me!"

9. "A _____ millimeter longer."

10. Here's how one product was pushed in 1963. Finish the jingle and you'll name the product. Then tell what was special about that year to that product.

        WE DON'T
        KNOW HOW
        TO SPLIT AN ATOM
        BUT AS TO WHISKERS
        LET US AT 'EM

        _____

11. What famous ad war between two companies revolved mainly around ashtrays?

12. Follow-up: Fill in the blanks in this ad headline, the first used in the counterattack in that war: "For years, _____ has been telling you _____ is _____ _____. Now we're going to tell you why."

13. What new Sixties product, destined to be a smash, began its attack on the American consciousness by advertising, "Help stamp out runny noses"?

14. "I'd rather fight than switch." Switch from what?

15. One of the most snickered-about slogans: "Had any lately?" Had any what?

SCORE _____ × **10 points each =**

_____ **(max. 150)**

What Do They Have in Common?

1. Richard Chamberlain and Vince Edwards.

2. Adam West and Burt Ward.

3. The Great Speckled Bird and The Kaleidoscope.

4. Natalie Wood & Robert Wagner and Janet Leigh & Tony Curtis.

5. Joe Bellino, John Huarte, Steve Spurrier, and Gary Beban.

6. Staughton Lynd, Herbert Aptheker, Tom Hayden. (Hint: A trip.)

7. Ramon George Sneyd, Paul Bridgman, Eric Starvo Galt, John Willard.

8. Rose Mary Woods and Evelyn Lincoln.

9. Low Memorial Library at Columbia, University Hall at Harvard, Willard Straight Hall at Cornell.

10. The three sisters of *Petticoat Junction*.

SCORE_____ × **10 points each =**
_____**(max. 100)**

●WHO THE HELL WAS LOUIS WASHKANSKY?

58
The Supreme Test

Questions for High Court watchers.

1. On June 17, 1963, the U.S. Supreme Court ruled that who couldn't do what to public school children?

2. And who led the legal battle that resulted in that decision?

3. Five Supreme Court associate justices ended their terms in the Sixties. Using their initials as clues, name them all.

F_____ F_____
T_____ C_____
C_____ W_____
A_____ G_____
A_____ F_____

4. And one chief justice, after surviving a recall struggle, called it quits: Earl Warren. Within two years, how old was he at retirement?

5. Two of Richard Nixon's Supreme Court nominees were rejected in the Sixties—the first in nearly 40 years. Who were they? (Spelling counts.)

SCORE_____ × **10 points each** =

_____**(max. 50)**

1

●WHO THE HELL WAS SARAH HUGHES?

59
Who Said?

Some choices in the first four; after that you're on your own.

1. "Those who make peaceful revolution impossible make violent revolution inevitable."
   - **A.** President Kennedy
   - **B.** J. Edgar Hoover
   - **C.** H. Rap Brown
   - **D.** Regis Debray
   - **E.** Chairman Mao

2. "And one path we shall never choose, and that is the path of surrender, or submission."
   - **A.** Nikita Khrushchev
   - **B.** Ahmed Ben Bella

   - **C.** Mark Rudd
   - **D.** Pope John XXIII
   - **E.** President Kennedy

3. "No more war. War never again."
   - **A.** David Ben-Gurion
   - **B.** Pope Paul VI
   - **C.** Bobby Kennedy
   - **D.** Leonid Brezhnev
   - **E.** Jomo Kenyatta

4. "I've been to the mountaintop."
   - **A.** Jean-Claude Killy
   - **B.** Timothy Leary
   - **C.** Thomas Merton
   - **D.** Martin Luther King
   - **E.** Maharishi Mahesh Yogi

5. "I was brainwashed."

6. "Colorless green ideas sleep furiously."

7. "Don't worry, I put notes behind all the pictures and they say, I shall return."

8. "Hello Muddah, hello Fadduh!"

9. "Ver-r-ry interesting!"

10. "You can't say Dallas hasn't been nice to you today."

11. "Another monk barbecue show."

12. "Holy barracuda!"

13. *"Vive le Québec libre!"*

14. *"Ich bin ein Berliner."*

15. *"Lass sie nach Berlin einkommen."*

16. "All I have I would have given gladly not to be standing here today."

17. "The police are not there to create disorder; they are there to maintain disorder."

18. "Keep the faith, baby!"

19. "When a Negro marries a white, the children are usually spotted."

20. "People ask me who my heroes are. I have only one: Hitler. . . . We need four or five Hitlers in Vietnam."

21. "We can see the light at the end of the tunnel."

22. "Some people see things as they are and ask why; I dream things that never were and ask why not?"

23. "The surface is fine and powdery."

24. "I'm an orphan of America. I live in Woodstock Nation."

25. "Segregation now, segregation tomorrow, segregation forever."

26. "Violence is necessary. It is as American as apple pie."

27. "I sleep each night a little better, a little more confidently, because Lyndon Johnson is my president."

28. ". . . these overeducated ivory-tower folks with pointed heads lookin' down their noses at you and me."

29. "Extremism in the defense of liberty is no vice . . . moderation in the pursuit of justice is no virtue."

30. (Referring to a crowd of 49 Nobel Prize winners) "This is the most extraordinary collection of talent . . . that has ever been gathered together at the White House—with the possible exception of when Thomas Jefferson dined alone."

SCORE_____ × **10 points each =**

_____ **(max. 300)**

60
One Little Word

The answer to each of these is a single word. Nice?

1. In *The Graduate,* Dustin Hoffman is told the key to the future lies in _____.

2. What's the word the young Helen Keller tries to say in the film *The Miracle Worker?*

3. Which university announced the reconstruction of a pre-Columbian map of the New World, indicating that Scandinavian sailors such as Leif Ericson probably discovered America before Columbus?

4. Clark Kerr's favorite word?

5. In a word, describe Jackie at the time of the November 1960 election.

6. Du Pont introduced a new "breathable" substitute for leather, used in shoes. They called it
   A. Du-Shu
   B. Nu-Shu
   C. Corfam
   D. Walltex

7. Name the Beatles' record company.

8. The first communications satellite was called _____.

9. In 1965 the State Department refused to let Bobby Fischer go to Havana for an international chess tournament. But Fischer played anyway. How? (Ten points extra credit: How did he do?)

10. According to the song by Herman's Hermits, Mrs. Brown had a lovely what?

11. A young singer's first TV special: *My Name Is* _____.

12. Barry McGuire somberly sang in '65 about "The Eve of _____."

13. What, according to Charles Schulz, is a warm puppy?

14. *The Group* was Mary McCarthy's story of eight _____ graduates.

15. First Communist nation visited by a U.S. President since World War II: _____.

16. What kind of troops did President Johnson send to Santo Domingo?

17. Resnais film: *La Guerre est* _____.

18. Crowd-control substance, sprayed from an aerosol can: _____.

19. The 1963 Sting Ray had a particularly noteworthy rear window. What was the name of this style?

20. How did Francis Chichester sail around the world? (Ten points extra credit: Name his craft.)

SCORE _____ × **10 points each** +

_____ **extra** = _____ **(max. 220)**

● WHO THE HELL WAS DR. HOWARD LEVY?

61
ING

1. _ I N G _ (Richard Starkey.)

2. _ _ _ _ I N G _ _ _ (Rubber-faced star of *Taste of Honey*.)

3. _ _ _ _ _ _ _ I N G (An organized unorganized event.)

4. _ I N G _ _ _ _ (What Mitch asked us to do.)

5. _ I N G - _ _ _ _ _ _ _ _ _ _ (High-flying stock.)

4 **SCORE**_____ × **10 points each** =

_____ **(max. 50)**

62
Quick Associations

Read down the list, and see what these entries make you think of. Just say the first thing that pops into your head, and then look up the answers to see if you're in the ball park.

1. The shape of a table
2. A woman named Viva
3. James "Groovy" Hutchinson
4. The word "camp"
5. Mudge, Stern, Baldwin, and Todd

6. Hump the Hostess
7. William Manchester
8. A park bench and a pocketbook used as a weapon
9. Alan Guttmacher
10. A hand named Thing
11. Clay Shaw
12. A TV commercial showing a little girl, flowers and a mushroom cloud
13. Reparations demands to churches
14. Illya Kuryakin
15. The Unisphere

SCORE_____ × **10 points each** =

_____**(max. 150)**

63
Author! Author!

Who wrote these Sixties big sellers? First, match five titles with male authors:

1. *JFK: The Man and the Myth*   Bob Hope

2. *I Owe Russia $1200*   Johnny Carson

3. *The Sot-Weed Factor*   Dan Greenburg

4. *Happiness Is a Dry Martini*   John Barth

5. *How to Be a Jewish Mother*   Victor Lasky

And now five by women:

6. *The American Way of Death*   Rachel Carson

7. *Sex and the College Girl*   Harper Lee

8. *Silent Spring*   Peg Bracken

9. *The I-Hate-to-Cook Book*   Jessica Mitford

10. *To Kill a Mockingbird*   Gael Greene

SCORE_____ × **10 points each** = _____(**max. 100**)

● WHO THE HELL WAS BARRY SADLER?

64
Openers

Identify the book from the opening words.

1. Call me Jonah.

2. Boys are playing basketball around a telephone pole with a backboard bolted to it.

3. If I am out of my mind, it's all right with me, thought Moses _____.

4. I met Jack Kennedy in November, 1946.

5. I swear 'fo God this is the cussingest' man ever born, he must've been cussing when he came into this world, when his mother, Miss Lillybelle Washington, gave birth to this heathen the first thing he said must've been a cuss word, he probably cussed out the midwife and his mother and anybody else who happened to be in sight, cussed them out for bringin' him into the world, he is that kind of man, you know.

SCORE_____ × **10 points each =**

_____**(max. 50)**

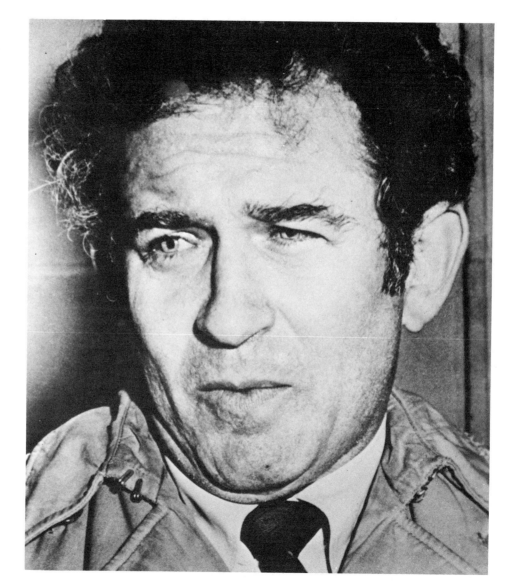

About Names

1. What was Che Guevara's first name?

2. "Hello, Dolly, well hello, Dolly, it's so nice to see you back where you belong." So what's your last name, Dolly? (Ten points extra credit for her maiden name.)

3. Johnson man W. W. Rostow was named for a literary light. Who? (Ten points extra credit: His brother, E. V. Rostow, was dean of Yale Law School. Whom was he named after?)

4. What was U Thant's first name?

5. The "H" in H. Rap Brown?

6. Last name of Mary, of Peter, Paul and Mary?

4

7. Do you know Eugene McCarthy's middle name?

8. Jazz saxophonist, last name Coleman?

9. Swimmer Schollander?

10. The first Mrs. George Wallace?

11. Do you know graphic designer Sister Corita's full name?

6

10

8

12. How about Dean Rusk's full name?

13. What does John Ronald Reuel mean?

14. Country Joe and the Fish—his last name, please?

12

15. How did Abbie Hoffman's name appear in court records?

16. What was the first name of Birdie of *Bye Bye Birdie?*

17. One book that got people up out of their chairs was *Miss Craig's 21-Day Shape-Up Program for Men and Women.* What was Miss Craig's first name?

18. Rod Steiger played Sol, who owned this shop in *The Pawnbroker*. What was Sol's last name? ▲

19. Mrs. Khrushchev's first name?

20. Here are Rosemary and her husband. What was their baby's name? (Ten points extra credit: What was their last name?) ◄

SCORE_____ × **10 points each +**

_____ **extra =** _____**(max. 230)**

66
Assassination Minutiae

1. Was Jackie sitting to the President's left or right in the car in Dallas?

2. To what hospital were JFK and Governor Connally rushed?
- **A.** Dallas Municipal
- **B.** Parkland Memorial
- **C.** Rose Hill
- **D.** Dallas Daughters of Mercy

3. The day JFK was shot the Dow-Jones industrial index dropped 21 points. When the stock exchange was back in operation the next Tuesday, the index
- **A.** dropped 12 points more
- **B.** dropped 22 points more
- **C.** stayed about even
- **D.** rose 32 points
- **E.** rose 11 points

4. Martin Luther King was assassinated on a motel balcony in Memphis. What motel?

5. What was he doing in Memphis?
- **A.** accepting an award
- **B.** inspecting a newly integrated school
- **C.** vacationing
- **D.** supporting a garbage collectors' strike

6. James Earl Ray was a fugitive abroad. Which of these countries was he *not* known to have visited?
- **A.** Canada
- **B.** England
- **C.** Portugal
- **D.** Italy

7. What hotel was Robert Kennedy shot in, and what was he doing there?

8. What was Sirhan Sirhan's middle name?

9. What occupation did Sirhan hope to follow?

10. In what city was Martin Luther King buried? (Ten points extra credit: Name the cemetery.)

SCORE_____ × **10 points each** =

_____**(max. 110)**

67
Song Fragments

Identify the song from the snippets supplied.

1. "Like a funeral pyre."

2. "Where have you gone, Joe Di-Maggio?"

3. "Chatting with a cheetah."

4. "Vera, Chuck and Dave."

5. "Every day in a letter."

And five from Dylan:

6. "The executioner's face."

7. "You'll sink like a stone."

8. "When the rooster crows."

9. "My big brass bed."

10. "I'm not sleepy."

SCORE_____ × 10 points each =

_____(max. 100)

68
A Half Quiz

Every other word is missing. Fill in the blanks. The quote, by the way, came from a president on national television.

"_____ shall _____ seek, _____ I _____ not _____, the _____ of _____ party _____ another _____ as _____ president."

SCORE_____ × 5 points each =

_____(max. 50)

● WHO THE HELL WAS MORTIMER CAPLIN?

69
Black Studies

1. What was Malcolm X's last name at birth?

2. What black man made history by filling Tom Clark's seat? (Ten points extra credit: What had he been doing just before that happened?)

3. He was a newspaper reporter, a State Department official, and American ambassador to Finland. He coauthored a book with Jackie Robinson. Then in 1964 he was tapped to head the United States Information Agency. Who was he?

4. Who sang, "I'm black and I'm proud," and how did he say it?

5. What was the name of the nurse Diahann Carroll played in her prece-

dent-setting 1968 TV series? And what was the nurse's marital status? (Ten points extra credit: What was the name of her son?)

6. James Baldwin's big books: *Nobody Knows* _____ _____, *Another* _____, *The Fire* _____ _____.

7

8

7. Who was Kelly Robinson's pal, Alexander Scott?

8. LeRoi Jones changed his name to _____?

9. Roy Wilkins delivered the eulogy, saying the killed man "believed in his country; it now remains to be seen whether his country believes in him." Not Martin. Who?

10. What happened at the Audubon Ballroom in New York City on Feb. 21, 1965?

SCORE_____ × **10 points each** +

_____**extra** = _____(**max. 120**)

70
Fill in the Blanks

1. On his way to the Massachusetts State Democratic Convention in 1964, Ted Kennedy suffered one of a long line of Kennedy mishaps: he broke his _____ in a _____ crash.

2. Fellini film: *La _____ _____*.

3. _____ _____ donated his modern sculpture collection to the new National Museum in Jerusalem.

4. President _____ _____ once concluded a radio-TV broadcast with the words, "We shall overcome."

5. _____ _____ William Calley.

6. _____ _____ read a poem in the cold at _____'s inaugural.

7. *The Electric Kool-Aid* _____ _____.

8. Fired Congolese premier: _____ Lumumba.

2

8

9. The 1964 version, at Berkeley, was the Free Speech Movement, involving protests over political activity; the 1965 remake was the _____ Speech Movement.

10. Blood, Sweat & Tears hit: "And When I'm _____."

SCORE_____ × 10 points each = _____ (max. 100)

● WHO THE HELL WAS VIOLA LIUZZO?

1. This dapper chap was busy with a nestful of birds in a popular 1966 film. What question was on many of their minds? ▲

2. If you were Frank Gallup, what would you call your boss?

3. With whom is this poor milkman probably conversing? ▶

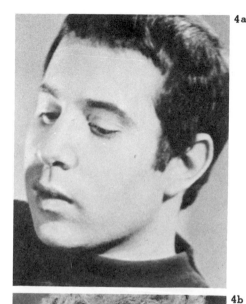

4a

4b

5

4. To whom did these two get down on their knees, begging her "please to come home"? ◄

5. What's this character probably chanting? ▲

SCORE _____ × **10 points each =**

_____ **(max. 50)**

● WHO THE HELL WAS JAMES FARMER?

93

In a Family Way

1. What was Mike McGear to Paul McCartney?

2. Mme. Ngo Dinh Nhu was the _____ of South Vietnam's President Ngo Dinh Diem.

3. They each scored with a big hit record in 1966: "Strangers in the Night" was his and "These Boots Are Made for Walking" was hers. Name the singers and tell their relationship.

4. Herbert and Bettina Aptheker were _____ and _____.

5. What famous person's son came back from Vietnam to report that 75 percent of enlisted men there were using marijuana?

SCORE_____ × **10 points each =**

_____ **(max. 50)**

● WHO THE HELL WAS LINDA LECLAIR?

73
More Sports–for the Hardcore

1. Off whom did Roger Maris hit No. 61?

2. Who stole second, third, and home in one inning in 1969?

3. How many NFL conference championships did Vince Lombardi win?

4. In 1960, Paul Hornung set the NFL points-in-a-single-season record. How many?

    A. 156   **C.** 166
    B. 160   **D.** 176

5. And in 1967, Sonny Jurgensen set the record for passes completed in a season. Pick it.

    A. 279   **C.** 291
    B. 288   **D.** 303

6. Only one team was named national college football champions three times in the Sixties. Which?

    A. Alabama   **C.** Texas
    B. Southern California   **D.** Michigan State

7. The Stanley Cup belonged to Canadians—either Montreal or Toronto—throughout the Sixties, save for one year: 1961. Who had it then?

8. Ara Parseghian coached Notre Dame. "Bear" Bryant coached Alabama. Tom Cahill coached _____.

9. Who won the 1968 U.S. Men's National tennis title? (Ten points extra credit: Who placed second?)

10. Match the World Series results with the years. (You need them all for your ten.)

    1960   Orioles over Dodgers, 4–0
    1962   Pirates over Yankees, 4–3
    1964   Tigers over Cardinals, 4–3
    1966   Yankees over Giants, 4–3
    1968   Cardinals over Yankees, 4–3eq,gv202,0

11. Who was the goat of the 1963 Series?

12. What was odd about Steve Barber's 1967 no-hit game?

13. First black Heisman Trophy winner, 1961: _____.

1

14. In the 1960 and 1961 Rose Bowl games, Big Ten teams Wisconsin and Minnesota went down to defeat at the hands of _____.

15. Who, in 1961, set an American League record for grand slam homers in a single season? How many?

16. In 1963, Bob Gibson tied the 58-year-old American League record for shutouts in one season. How many?

17. Who was the first major league pitcher to strike out 19 in a nine-inning game?

18. Except for one tie game (called for rain in the ninth), the National League won every Sixties All-Star Game but one. What year was that, and where was it played? (Ten points extra credit if you recall the score.)

19. Who followed Wilt Chamberlain's spectacular seven-year rule as top NBA scorer by leading the league in the 1966–67 season?

20. What do these ten men have in common: Ron Hansen, Don Schwall, Tom Tresh, Gary Peters, Tony Oliva, Curt Blefary, Tommie Agee, Rod Carew, Stan Bahnsen, Lou Piniella?

21. Who led the National League in batting *three* times in the Sixties?
   A. Tommy Davis   **C.** Roberto Clemente
   B. Pete Rose

22. And who led that league in home runs three times in the decade?
   A. Willie Mays   **C.** Willie McCovey
   B. Hank Aaron

23. Whom did the middle-aged Pancho Gonzales defeat in a grueling five-hours-plus match in 1965, the amazing score being 22–24, 1–6, 16–14, 6–3, 11–9?

24. Y. A. Tittle completed 221 passes for 3,145 yards in 1963, his second-to-last season. What was his *full* name?

25. Two members of the Detroit Pistons grabbed more than 1,000 rebounds during the 1960–61 season. Initials B. H. and W. D. Name them.

SCORE_____ × **10 points each** + _____**extra** = _____**(max. 270)**

74
Explain

1. "Where were you when the lights went out?"

2. AuH_2O.

3. When the TV performers' union, AFTRA, went out on strike in 1967, half the Huntley-Brinkley team worked, half didn't. Which one worked? Explain.

4. "There is nothing that would lift him more than for us to win in November. And I say, let us _____." Complete the quote and explain.

5. "The ugliest thing I ever saw," said the President. (Ten points extra credit: Who had a right to feel insulted by the presidential putdown?)

SCORE_____ $\times$ **10 points each** +

_____ **extra** = _____ **(max. 60)**

3

Just Eyes

If you're good at identifying faces, this one is a bit tougher: you get only the eyes. As a little bit of help we're letting you know who ten are: Adlai Stevenson, Hubert Humphrey, Hugh Downs, Jim Nabors, Elliott Gould, Spencer Tracy, Roy Wilkins, William F. Buckley, Jr., Whitney Young, Jr., Helen Reddy

1. _____   13. _____
2. _____   14. _____
3. _____   15. _____
4. _____   16. _____
5. _____   17. _____
6. _____   18. _____
7. _____   19. _____
8. _____   20. _____
9. _____
10. _____
11. _____
12. _____

SCORE_____ × **10 points each** =

_____ **(max. 200)**

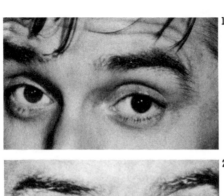

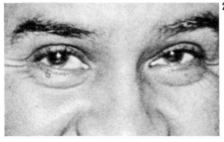

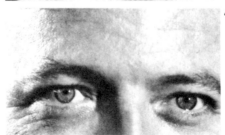

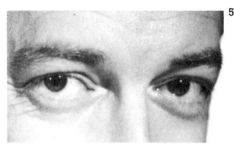

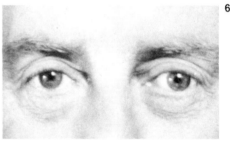

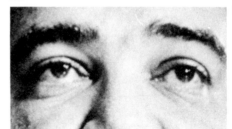

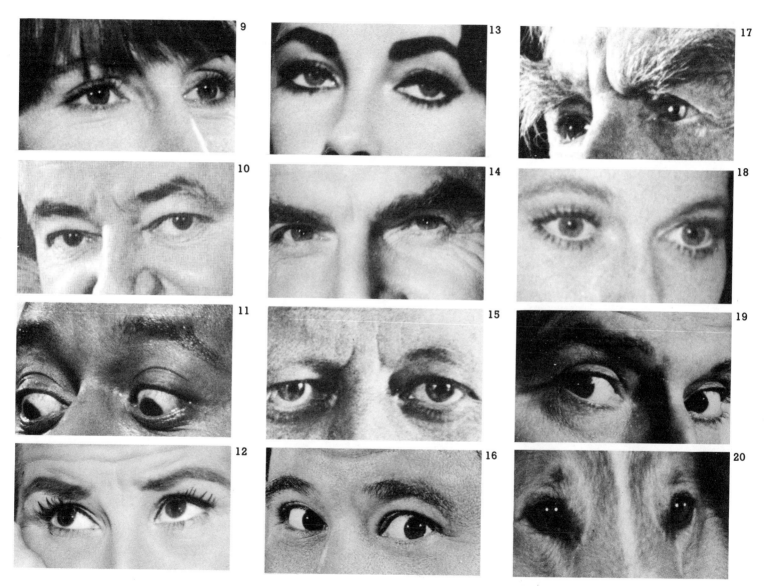

● WHO THE HELL WAS LEONARD WEINGLASS?

76
Special Mystery Photo

These three are sisters, rarely photographed together. Their father was an important world leader at the time this photo was taken, in July 1964. It's so hard to guess, you get 30 points just for coming up with the family name.

(Ten points extra credit for each of the first names you know.)

SCORE 30 points + _____ **extra =**

_____ **(max. 60)**

77
A Hairy Test

Behold: The Ten Best Coiffured Women of 1963! Who were they? You need six right for the basic ten points, and there are ten points extra credit for each extra identification.

SCORE 10 points for 6 right +

_____ **extra =** _____ **(max. 50)**

78
Health and Welfare

1. How was thalidomide used?

2. It was published in 1966 and is almost universally known as Masters and Johnson. What was it really called?

3. What was the TV series *The Eleventh Hour* about?

4. Hubert Humphrey served as acting President for a few hours in 1965, while LBJ underwent surgery. What kind?

5. Remember the Phoenix woman, hostess of a local *Romper Room* series, who made headlines when she flew to Sweden in 1962? Why, exactly, did she go? (Ten points extra credit for remembering her name, too.)

6. What was Krebiozen?

7. What did Dr. Herman Taller have to say about calories?

8. Who called his slimming routine *The Doctor's Quick Weight Loss Diet?*

9. What's the regimen that called for gradually reducing the daily diet to nothing but brown rice?

10. The Surgeon General's 1964 report concluded—as if you don't know—that smoking is hazardous to your health. Name that Surgeon General.

SCORE_____ × **10 points each +**

_____**extra** = _____**(max. 110)**

● WHO THE HELL WAS CLAUDIA JOHNSON?

Multiple Choice

1. What rock group popularized the jerk?

   A. The Monkees
   B. The Rolling Stones
   C. The Who
   D. The Electric Grape
   E. The Everly Brothers

2. Who was named the first honorary citizen of the U.S.A.?

   A. Queen Elizabeth
   B. Harold Macmillan
   C. Albert Schweitzer
   D. Winston Churchill
   E. Yuri Gagarin

3. Which state had the first lottery since 1894?

   A. Massachusetts
   B. New Hampshire
   C. New York
   D. Nevada
   E. Kentucky

4. The ship that ran aground on *Gilligan's Island* was named

   A. *Denver*
   B. *Minnow*
   C. *Jennifer*
   D. *Maynard G. Krebs*
   E. *Oded*

5. In 1966, Roman Catholics were told

   A. the Pope had had a vision of a world at peace
   B. daily mass would be mandatory
   C. meat abstinence would be optional
   D. confessions could be in the vernacular
   E. the Orthodox should be tolerated

6. What was the dance that began among Baltimore blacks and became a brief craze in 1960?

   A. Watusi
   B. Frug
   C. Madison
   D. Twist
   E. Washboard

4

7. What bridge did Bobbie Gentry sing about in her hit, "Ode to Billie Joe"?
- **A.** Golden Gate
- **B.** London
- **C.** Tallahatchie
- **D.** Old
- **E.** Nashville

8. What name was given to the huge campsite in Washington at the 1968 Poor People's Campaign?
- **A.** Johnsonville
- **B.** Poor People's City
- **C.** Resurrection City
- **D.** Abernathy Heights
- **E.** Washington Flats

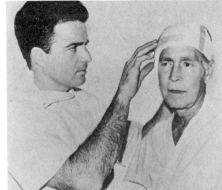

9. Can you pick Dr. Kildare's hospital?
- **A.** County General
- **B.** Harrison Memorial
- **C.** Blair General
- **D.** Dommu General
- **E.** Eastern

10. And, from the same group, Ben Casey's hospital?

11. Who coined the phrase "black power"?
- **A.** Stokely
- **B.** Rap
- **C.** Malcolm
- **D.** Eldridge
- **E.** Ali

12. Bay of Pigs prisoners were released by the Cubans in time for
- **A.** Christmas
- **B.** New Year's Day

C. Fourth of July
D. Election Day
E. Dean Rusk's birthday

13. James Pike

A. Tried to contact his dead father and later died in a car crash in Death Valley

B. tried to contact his dead wife and later died of a brain tumor

C. tried to contact Jesus and later died swimming

D. tried to contact his dead son and later died following a fall in the Judean desert

E. tried to contact various dead relatives and is still alive

14. Who was shot in a Chicago apartment with Fred Hampton?

A. Mark Rudd
B. Bobby Seale
C. Dick Gregory
D. Harlan Shabazz
E. Mark Clark

15. Who was Sam Sheppard's lawyer?

A. Louis Nizer
B. F. Lee Bailey
C. William Kunstler
D. Archibald Cox
E. Melvin Belli

16. Jean-Paul Sartre declined

A. the Nobel Prize
B. the French Academy's Medal of Honor
C. the National Book Award
D. the Prix Goncourt
E. all of the above

17. Where did Truman Capote's *In Cold Blood* take place?

A. Fullerton, Calif.
B. Palos Verdes, Calif.
C. Garden City, Kan.
D. Shawnee Mission, Kan.
E. Morris, Conn.

18. The correct name of the Woodstock festival of 1969 was

A. the Woodstock Music and Art Fair
B. the Woodstock Music Fest
C. the Woodstock Pop, Rock, and Soul Festival
D. Woodstock 1969
E. Woodstock!

19. What kind of exam did Teddy Kennedy supposedly cheat on at Harvard?

A. English
B. calculus
C. American history
D. differential equations
E. Spanish

20. In Chicago this smiler was sentenced to jail for ▶

A. perjury
B. conspiracy
C. contempt
D. weapons-law violation
E. littering

21. Who did the "beach movies" series?

A. Annette Funicello and Bobby Darin
B. Annette Funicello and Frankie Avalon
C. Darlene Gillespie and Cubby O'Brien
D. Doris Day and Tony Curtis
E. Shari Lewis and Tommy Sands

22. Where did Mariner II go in 1962?

A. Mars
B. Venus
C. Around the moon twice and home
D. Around the moon once and home
E. To Venus, Mercury, and the Sun

20

24

25. What house does the moon have to be in for the Age of Aquarius to begin?

    A. The big house
    B. The front house
    C. The other house
    D. The seventh house
    E. The ninth house

SCORE_____ × **10 points each** +

_____**extra** = _____**(max. 260)**

23. Where did we pick up the expression, "Would you believe . . . ?"

    A. Buick commercials
    B. Walter Cronkite
    C. David Brinkley
    D. *Get Smart*
    E. Joan Baez

24. How was Dag Hammarskjöld killed? (Ten points extra credit: What country?)

    A. Sniper
    B. Plane crash
    C. Apartment fire
    D. Snake bite
    E. Acute indigestion and complications

80
Odd One Out

1. Which *wasn't* the name of a U.S. missile?
   - **A.** *Atlas*
   - **B.** *Titan*
   - **C.** *Jupiter*
   - **D.** *Hound Dog*
   - **E.** *Davy Crockett*
   - **F.** *Baby*
   - **G.** *Hawk*
   - **H.** *Sidewinder*

2. Who *didn't* die in the Sixties?
   - **A.** Douglas MacArthur
   - **B.** James Dean
   - **C.** Robert Frost
   - **D.** Gracie Allen

3

3. Which Kennedyana statement *isn't* true?
   - **A.** JFK won a Pulitzer Prize.
   - **B.** Jackie was several months older than Jack.
   - **C.** Bobby was in Washington when his brother was shot.

4. Which work of art *didn't* visit the U.S.A. during the Sixties?
   - **A.** *Whistler's Mother*
   - **B.** *Mona Lisa*
   - **C.** *Pietà*
   - **D.** *Venus de Milo*

5. Who *didn't* win a Nobel Peace Prize?
   - **A.** Linus Pauling
   - **B.** Bertrand Russell
   - **C.** Dag Hammarskjöld
   - **D.** Martin Luther King
   - **E.** René Cassin

3

6. Which *didn't* Andy Warhol paint?
A. Campbell's chicken with rice soup
B. Del Monte freestone peach halves
C. Brillo
D. Fox's U-Bet chocolate syrup

7. Who *didn't* invade Czechoslovakia in 1968?
A. Bulgaria
B. Poland
C. East Germany
D. Romania
E. Hungary

8. Which silly title *wasn't* a Sixties hit?
A. "Da Doo Ron Ron"
B. "Shimmy Shimmy Koko Bop"
C. "Ob La Di"
D. "Do Wah Diddy Diddy"
E. "Alley Oop"

9. Who *didn't* write a book about the Kennedy years?
A. Evelyn Lincoln
B. Pierre Salinger
C. Arthur Schlesinger
D. Richard Nixon
E. Ted Sorensen

10. Which city *didn't* have a major riot?
A. New York
B. Los Angeles
C. Chicago
D. Newark
E. Detroit
F. Washington
G. Baltimore
H. Kansas City
I. Cleveland
J. Oakland

SCORE_____ × **10 points each** =

_____**(max. 100)**

81
And Then They Grew Up

Who are these youthful fellows?

2. That's Charlie, the Welsh terrier. ▶
Who's the kid?

1. His teeth improved as he aged. ▲

3. Andy's pal, with rolled pantleg and bare middle. He stayed cute. ▶

4

4. A couple of famous sons and a
◄ friend. They liked to sing after school.

5. Rob and Laura are having a heart-to-heart with their son. Obviously a heavy conversation. Who's the little guy? (Twenty points extra credit for knowing the character's *middle* name.)▼

SCORE_____ × **10 points each** +

_____**extra** = _____ **(max. 70)**

5

82
Farewells

1. Can you give the year—within two —when Bob Cousy retired from active play? (Ten points extra credit: With what team did he try a brief playing comeback some years later?)

2. Why did Tom Clark leave the Supreme Court?

3. One of the best-publicized retirements of the decade was that of a boat. A British boat. A big British boat. Name it.

4. Another big Sixties farewell went to John Charles Daly and crew. Why was that?

5. What President of a country offered to resign in 1967 but changed his mind when massive street demonstrations supported him?

6. After the 1967 military coup in Greece, King Constantine staged a counter-coup, failed to regain power, and

    A. was executed by a firing squad
    B. was imprisoned
    C. fled to Italy
    D. was exiled to Corfu

7. To where did Eldridge Cleaver split?

8

10

10. Why did Fred Friendly resign as president of CBS-TV News?

SCORE_____ × **10 points each** +

_____**extra** = _____(max. 120)

8. And where did Jack Paar go after his spat with the NBC censor? (Ten points extra credit: What was the tiff about?)

9. What basketball giant announced his retirement early in 1960, then changed his mind and signed another contract?

The Honors Test

A connoisseur's quiz, with tough questions appropriately weighted at 20 points each. No time limit, but please don't ask a friend for help.

1. What was Benjamin's last name in *The Graduate?*

2. James Earl Ray maintained he was following orders from a mysterious Latin. Name this mystery man, and tell what color hair Ray said the man had.

3. Whose name meant He Who Enlightens?

4. For what is Hibbing, Minn., famous?

5. In Miami Beach in 1968 the Deauville served as Reagan headquarters. In which hotel was the victorious Nixon camp?

6. What did Winston Churchill break on June 28, 1962?
  A. His thighbone
  B. The longevity record for British prime ministers
  C. Book sales records for Britain
  D. His left foot
  E. A historic vase at Buckingham Palace

7. In 1969 the daughter of a wealthy Florida businessman was kidnapped and buried alive for more than 80 hours in a box near Atlanta. Name her.

8. What famous statue in a harbor was damaged in 1964? How? And where?

9. *David and Lisa* was one of those films of the Sixties it was popular to see more than once. The picture was adapted from a story by psychiatrist Theodore Isaac Rubin. What was his title for the tale of David and Lisa?

10. Where did the first Peace Corps recruits take their training? (Twenty points extra credit: Where did they then serve?)

11. Who said, "Let's get this goddamn thing airborne!"

12. Name President Kennedy's personal physician.

13. What was Charles Manson's middle initial?

14. In what room did Arlo Guthrie see the psychiatrist in the song "Alice's Restaurant"?

19. Choose John Glenn's middle name:

    A. Herschel
    B. Herman
    C. Michael
    D. Jeremy
    E. Charleston

20. Who was Marni Nixon?

SCORE_____ × **20 points each** +

_____**extra** = _____**(max. 420)**

15. At 14, Prince Charles had half of England cluck-clucking and half saying, "Jolly good show" when he stopped at a pub and had a little nip. A nip of what?

16. Where is this toothy chap making such a scene? ▶

17. "What're we fightin' for?" is part of the refrain of a popular Sixties antiwar tune. You may be able to sing it, but can you name it accurately?

18. In 1962, Studebaker introduced a neat new model. Name it.

84
But...

Another tough quiz to show you that, yes, you do know a lot but there are always things you *don't* know. Thirty points each.

1. You know all about the first successful coronary transplant—the patient, the doctor, the location. *But* can you name the 24-year-old woman whose heart was used?

2. You know JFK said, "Ask not what your country can do for you—ask what you can do for your country." *But* can you give the five words preceding this quote?

3. You know Richard Nixon said, "You won't have Nixon to kick around any more because, gentlemen, this is my last press conference." *But* do you know what he said just before that?

4. You know that Lee Harvey Oswald, presumably, killed President Kennedy in 1963. *But* what did another Oswald—Oswald Pick—do in 1966?

5. You know that Lee Oswald shot from the Texas School Book Depository. *But* do you know what floor? And which window?

SCORE_____ × 30 points each =

_____(max. 150)

5

3

● WHO THE HELL WAS EMMETT GROGAN?

85
For High Honors

Now, for those who care to test the very best: tougher still. *Forty* points each. You may bring an expert into the booth.

1. Who first said, "Don't trust anyone over 30," and how old was he at the time?

2. Svetlana Alliluyeva, Stalin's daughter, defected to the West in 1967. In what city did she first ap-proach the U.S. embassy, and why was she given permission to go there in the first place?

3. An assistant secretary of agriculture was fired for having accepted favors from Billie Sol Estes. What was his name?

4. What was Lee Harvey Oswald's nickname in the Marines?

5. Who was Dr. Donald Goldecker?

6. Who was Captain Christopher Pike?

7. Name President Johnson's personal secretary and personal physician.

8. What was *You're in the Picture?*

13

12

14. When the Selective Service went to a national lottery for choosing eligible men, what was the first date drawn?

15. Who ran the First Annual All Ivy League and Seven Sisters Trivia Contest, at Columbia University, and then wrote *Trivia,* launching the nationwide Trivia quiz fad of the Sixties?

SCORE_____ × **40 points each =**

_____ **(max. 600)**

9. "The Soccer War" was an undeclared conflict between Honduras and El Salvador, the result of a riot following a close soccer match between teams of the two Latin American nations. Who won the crucial game, by what score?

10. Who produced *Konga* and what was his biggest claim to fame?

11. By what name was the Singing Nun known around the convent?

12. What were the names of the two night clubs Jack Ruby owned in Dallas?

13. In September 1963 a tree was chopped down at Rutgers University. It was a 68-foot, 160-year-old white oak. Why did that get a lot of attention?

10

● WHO THE HELL WAS ABIGAIL FOLGER?

86
Final Potpourri

Last chance to lift your score.

1. What did Jack Newfield call his study of the New Left?

2. Barbie found a boyfriend, a best girlfriend, and even a black chum in the Sixties. Name them all.

3. When he hung up his uniform for the last time, he could boast of having won baseball's MVP award how many times? ▼

3

4

8

4. Who they?▲

5. Where did Bull Connor call home? (Ten points extra credit for knowing his first name.)

6. What actor did Lynda Bird Johnson date before she got serious with Chuck?

7. How many ballots did the Democrats take to nominate JFK in 1960?

8. Which came first: Nixon's first presidential win or Julie's marriage?

9. Who were Julia's coauthors on *Mastering the Art of French Cooking?* (Both of them)

10. What did Neil Sedaka say breakin' up is?

11. What did Mark Lane call his book about the Kennedy assassination?

12. Whom does Jesus love "more than you will know"?

13. What was Buzz Aldrin's first name?

14. With whom do you associate Stanyan Street?

15. What hard-to-eat food was honored by having a woman's hairstyle named after it?

SCORE_____ × **10 points each +**

_____**extra** = _____**(max. 160)**

● WHO THE HELL WAS SAM THE PLUMBER?

A_ _SW_ _S

1
Who?

1. Yuri A. Gagarin
2. R. Sargent Shriver
3. Albert Finney
4. Gandalf
5. Ted Kennedy, in his 1962 Massachusetts race for the Senate
6. Potter Stewart
7. Pope John XXIII
8. Newton N. Minow
9. Walter Jenkins
10. Vaughn Meader
11. The Red Guard
12. Truman Capote (Extra credit: *Washington Post* publisher Kay Graham)
13. V. K. Krishna Menon
14. James Meredith
15. Benjamin Spock *(Baby and Child Care)*
16. Claes Oldenburg
17. William Sloane Coffin
18. Tippi Hedrin
19. Timothy Leary (See the group's initials? Get it?)
20. Dow Chemical Company
21. Otto Kerner
22. Clark Kerr, president of the University of California
23. Soviet delegate Valerian Zorin
24. Rudolf Nureyev
25. (Pope) Paul VI, whose 1964 trip to the Holy Land was the first by a pope since St. Peter
26. Thomas Dodd (Extra credit: Drew Pearson and Jack Anderson)
27. Bertrand Russell
28. George Murphy
29. Ken Kesey
30. Desmond Morris

● **Who the Hell Was Abraham Zapruder?** Lucky home-movie maker who filmed the JFK assassination and sold the flick for a small bundle

2
What?

1. Mrs. F. gave birth to quintuplets—a boy and four girls
2. Stole away the Braves baseball team
3. They were lost at sea (submarines)
4. She returned to the Metropolitan Opera, ending her six-year dispute with Met general manager Rudolf Bing
5. Made color-print film rolls generally available
6. They were suspended from NFL play for betting on league games
7. They had their silver content eliminated, switching to a "sandwich" of copper between layers of cupronickel
8. Joined forces for *Julie and Carol at Carnegie Hall,* the most memorable TV variety special of the year
9. He was voted out of the House of Representatives

10. The patron saint of travelers was dropped from the Catholic Church's list of recognized saints because his origins and even his existence were deemed uncertain (St. Valentine suffered the same fate)
11. Handed over to her the Miss America crown
12. He and his ship, the *Pueblo,* were captured by North Koreans
13. It completed the first undersea voyage around the world
14. The DeSoto was discontinued by the Chrysler Corporation
15. They didn't merge, despite an earlier announcement that a marriage was under consideration

● **Who the Hell Was Daniel Burros?** Ku Klux Klanner who killed himself when it was revealed that he was Jewish

3
Where?

1. Argentina
2. Bethel, N.Y.
3. University of California at Berkeley
4. Seattle, for the 1962 World's Fair
5. E—Arlington
6. Londonderry
7. Squaw Valley, Calif.
8. Chicago, Berkeley, and New York
9. Birmingham
10. The University of Alabama
11. Darien

12. My Lai

13. A houseboat

14. Algiers Motel (the book: *The Algiers Motel Incident*)

15. D—Guatemala

16. Burbank

17. Bates Motel

18. The Beatles (all are mentioned in songs)

19. The LBJ Ranch

20. The Astrodome, in Houston

21. Winchester Cathedral

22. Ryman Auditorium (Nashville)

23. C—17 Cherry Tree Lane (*Mary Poppins*)

24. Idlewild International Airport

25. Glassboro, N.J.

● **Who the Hell Was Max Yasgur?** Dairy farmer whose turf was used for the Woodstock fest

4
Why?

1. He was being escorted, against his will, from the floor of the 1964 Republican National Convention in San Francisco, as NBC viewers witnessed

2. Silver certificates, because they, unlike the new federal reserve notes, could be turned in for silver

3. On *The Fugitive*, Dr. Richard Kimble (played by David Janssen) ran from Inspector Gerard (played by Barry Morse), who thought he (R. K.) had killed his (R. K.'s) wife; he hadn't

4. He didn't meet the mental standards

5. It ran 90 minutes each week (Extra credit: ranch foreman; Shiloh Ranch in Wyoming)

● **Who the Hell Was Regis Philbin?** Joey Bishop's sidekick on his late night show

5.
When?

1. 1965

2. 1961

3. 1964

4. 1965

5. 1967

6. D and G were in 1959, J was in 1970; the rest are Sixties events (Can you believe it?)

● **Who the Hell Was Carl Oglesby?** President of SDS in 1965–1966 and leftist writer

6
Dates

1. Moratorium Day, Oct. 15, 1969

2. Tet Offensive, Jan. 29, 1968

3. Beatles' last American concert, Aug. 29, 1966

4. First moon walk, July 20, 1969

5. President Johnson's no-run announcement, Mar. 31, 1968

7
Salutes

1. John-John Kennedy, at his father's funeral

2. R-r-right here on our stage, on Ed Sullivan's TV show

3. A nun

4. The photo of the *Pueblo* crew being held captive by the North Koreans

5. As given by *Star Trek*'s Mr. Spock, the best-known of all Vulcans, it's a raised hand, palm out, fingers paired off and split into a single "V" (Extra credit: "Live long and prosper!")

8
Who Came Before?

1. John Diefenbaker

2. J. Edward Day

3. Lal Bahadur Shastri

4. Dave Garroway

5. W. Averell Harriman

● **Who the Hell Was Mario Savio?** Leader of the Free Speech Movement at Berkeley, 1964

9
Phrasemaking

1. freedom ride
2. moral decay
3. participatory democracy
4. pillbox hat
5. military-industrial complex
6. flower children
7. Day-Glo paint
8. guerrilla theater
9. rat fink
10. missile gap
11. Bass Weejuns
12. pot party
13. white backlash
14. peace feeler
15. Great Society
16. talking blues
17. nonverbal communication
18. rice paddy
19. jug band
20. cultural revolution
21. generation gap
22. pop art
23. computer dating
24. elephant joke
25. topless bathing suit
26. Tet offensive
27. credibility gap
28. fascist pig
29. mellow yellow
30. fun fur
31. New Frontier
32. good vibes
33. silent majority
34. head shop
35. greasy kid stuff

● **Who the Hell Was Fannie Lou Hamer?** Mississippi civil rights leader, big in voter registration

10
Slogan Power!

1. People!
2. Pigs!
3. Or mutilate!
4. Drop out!
5. We won't go!
6. Johnson!
7. Not war!
8. You know he's right!
9. How many kids did you kill today?
10. NLF is going to win!
11. Watching!
12. The one!
13. The wall, motherfuckers!
14. Huey Newton, Black Panther leader
15. Own thing

11
It Pays to Increase Your Word Power

1. Julie Andrews, in the 1964 Disney film *Mary Poppins*
2. The movement for improved conditions for Chicano migratory farmworkers
3. Payola
4. Honorable
5. Acid
6. Trashing
7. Be-in
8. Nonbook
9. Radical chic
10. Law and order

● **Who the Hell Was Leslie Hornby?** Twiggy

12
Compare and Contrast

1. Marguerite was Lee Oswald's mother, Marina his wife
2. Alinsky without the *W* was a community organizer, with the *W* a Bobby Kennedy adviser
3. Grayson was president of Columbia University, Claude was governor of Florida
4. Groppi was a priest (Milwaukee's open-housing father), Pike an Episcopal bishop; both were troublemakers, both resigned

5. Shelton was a Ku Klux Klan imperial wizard, Scheer edited the muck-raking *Ramparts* magazine

6. According to the courts, Whitmore didn't kill the New York career girls, Janice Wylie and Emily Hoffert; Robles did

7. Robert founded the John Birch Society, Joseph counseled the Army during the McCarthy hearings in the Fifties

8. Of English street types, mods were snazzily attired, reasonably refined, and articulate; rockers were the motorcycle-and-leather-boot set

9. Sam was a doctor jailed for killing his wife and set free as innocent years later, Alan was the astronaut who first traveled in space—for a trip of 116 miles

10. S. Y. Agnon was the Israeli Nobel literature laureate; if you don't know who Agnew was, you're reading the wrong book

13
And One to Throw You for a Loop

1. Joey Dee sang "Peppermint Twist" (with the Starlighters)
2. Bobby Vee sang "Devil or Angel"
3. The Bee Gees sang "Massachusetts"
4. B. B. King sang "Sweet 16"
5. Dee Clark sang "Raindrops" (on the Vee Jay label)

● **Who the Hell Was Jean Shrimpton?** Top fashion model

14
High Fashion... and Low

1. British designer Mary Quant
2. Rudi Gernreich
3. Monokini
4. An Uncle Sam suit
5. *Bonnie and Clyde*
6. *Cleopatra* started women wearing "the Cleopatra look" in everything from jewelry to hairdos
7. Jackie Kennedy
8. Nehru and Mao
9. Love beads
10. C—Priscilla of Boston

15
Glorious Food

1. *Candy*
2. Chocolate cake
3. Ho Chi Minh
4. C—cats and dogs
5. The Mashed Potato (Extra credit: "Mashed Potato Time")

● **Who the Hell Was Mandy Rice-Davies?** Christine Keeler's sidekick in England's Profumo scandal

16
Memorable Marriages

1. Nelson Rockefeller (and wags were singing, "Forget your troubles, come on get Happy . . .")
2. On Johnny Carson's *Tonight* show (they're Tiny Tim and Miss Vicky)
3. Beatle George Harrison
4. On the Greek island of Skorpios
5. The White House, which was the proper place for the groom of Luci Baines Johnson
6. David Harris, famous for burning his draft card
7. It might—she was the American student who married Crown Prince Palden Thondup Namgyal of Sikkim in 1963 (Extra credit: Sarah Lawrence)
8. So it was his 13th marriage (11th wife)
9. John Lennon and Yoko Ono
10. Captain
11. Harry Karl (Extra credit: shoes)
12. Connie Stevens
13. Gamble Benedict; Romanian (Extra credit: Andrei Porumbeanu)
14. Jackie Hyde
15. Priscilla Ann Beaulieu

● **Who the Hell Was Norman F. Dacey?** Author of *How to Avoid Probate*

17
Television

1. Mayberry
2. Johnny Carson; *Tonight*
3. A—Tramp
4. The shooting of Lee Oswald by Jack Ruby
5. Jacqueline
6. Jackie Kennedy breathed her way through a tour of the White House ("This is the Blue Room. . . . The walls are blue!")
7. It's the Smothers Brothers; Tom played guitar, Dick the string bass
8. Alger Hiss
9. Leslie Uggams
10. Rob and Laura Petrie of *The Dick Van Dyke Show*
11. Lurch
12. *The Rogues*
13. Ann Sothern (Extra credit: 1928 Porter)
14. Clampett
15. "Harvest of Shame"
16. "By Henry Gibson," of course
17. *The Untouchables*
18. Stalag 13, on *Hogan's Heroes*
19. McHale's Navy; Captain Binghamton (Joe Flynn)
20. The weekly televised news conference featuring Senate minority leader Everett Dirksen and House Republican leader Charles Halleck; it was not big in the ratings
21. *Car 54, Where Are You?*
22. D—His shoe
23. Dean Jagger, the principal (Extra credit: Jefferson High)
24. Skitch Henderson
25. From 12 o'clock, clockwise: David Jones, Mickey Dolenz, Mike Nesmith, Peter Tork—known collectively as the Monkees (Extra credit: They made only one film, *Head*)

● **Who the Hell Was Emily Hoffert?** Victim, with Janice Wylie, in New York City's "career girl murders" case

18
Philosophy and Faith

1. *Time*
2. Maharishi Mahesh Yogi
3. Herbert Marcuse
4. Luci Johnson became a Roman Catholic
5. Young girls picked them, every one (When will they ever learn?)
6. Yes, he was
7. Jacqueline Grennan, then Sister Jacqueline (Extra credit: Webster College in Webster Grove, Mo.)
8. Tom Lehrer, in "The Vatican Rag"
9. Pope Paul VI visited Yankee Stadium
10. Pope Paul VI and Orthodox Patriarch Athenagoras were seeking to take the first steps toward healing the 900-year-old schism between their churches

● **Who the Hell Was Dr. Carl Coppolino?** New Jersey anesthesiologist acquitted of murdering the husband of his onetime mistress and convicted of murdering his first wife, Carmela

19
If You Can't Answer This One, the Whole Decade Was a Waste

"Good night, Dick" (Rowan and Martin *Laugh-In* routine)

20
Alphabet

1. J—author of *The Sensuous Woman*
2. M—boss of Agent 007
3. O—heroine of *The Story of O* by Pauline Reage
4. *V*—novel by Thomas Pynchon
5. *Z*—Costa-Gavras movie

21
A/K/A

1. Carl Yastrzemski
2. The Beatles
3. Eugene McCarthy
4. Wilt Chamberlain
5. Wilt Chamberlain again
6. General William Westmoreland
7. Cassius Clay
8. John Coltrane
9. Konrad Adenauer
10. Oh, come on!

● **Who the Hell Was Ronald L. Ridenhour?** Viet vet whose letters led to the investigation of the My Lai massacre

22
The Movies

1. *The Sound of Music* (the woman, of course, is Julie Andrews, singing, "The hills are alive with the sound of music")

2. *Funny Girl* (1968)

3. Doris Day and Rock Hudson

4. B—Stockholm

5. Trevor Howard and Marlon Brando did it—costarred as William Bligh and Fletcher Christian in *Mutiny on the Bounty*

6. *G*eneral, *M*ature, *R*estricted, *X*

7. *I Am Curious (Yellow)*

8. Sleeping (the film was *Sleep*)

9. Wrote the novel that became the first *Planet of the Apes* movie

10. C—direct

11. Spillane himself

12. *The Hustler, Hemingway's Adventures of a Young Man* and *Hombre*

13. *It's a Mad, Mad, Mad, Mad World*

14. Ghidra, the three-headed; Dogora, the giant jellyfish; Gamera, the toothed turtle; Ebirah, the colossal crab; Gyaos, the fanged flying fox

15. Sue Lyon

16. *Exodus*, Otto Preminger

17. Merkin Muffley (Extra credit: "How I Stopped Worrying and Learned to Love the Bomb")

18. "A Space Odyssey"

19. Mary Tyler Moore

20. *Darling*

21. A–H, B–I, C–F, D–J, E–G

22. Charles Bronson, James Coburn, Robert Vaughn, Horst Buchholz, Brad Dexter

23. **A.** *The Apartment*, 1960
    J. *West Side Story*, 1961
    C. *Lawrence of Arabia*, 1962
    I. *Tom Jones*, 1963
    F. *My Fair Lady*, 1964
    H. *The Sound of Music*, 1965
    D. *A Man for All Seasons*, 1966
    B. *In the Heat of the Night*, 1967
    G. *Oliver!*, 1968
    E. *Midnight Cowboy*, 1969

24. Each won *two* Best Actress awards—Hepburn for *Guess Who's Coming to Dinner?* and *The Lion in Winter*, Taylor for *Butterfield 8* and *Who's Afraid of Virginia Woolf?*

25. *The Ten Commandments*, 1956

26. "We blew it"

27. Raquel Welch

28. *Breakfast at Tiffany's, The Sandpiper, Butch Cassidy and the Sundance Kid*

29. Sidney Poitier; *Lilies of the Field*

30. *West Side Story;* George Chakiris and Rita Moreno won for supporting roles, Jerome Robbins and Robert Wise shared the directorial award, and the film took Best Picture as well

● **Who the Hell Was Arnold Zenker?** TV exec who read news during 1967 AFTRA strike, subbing for Walter Cronkite

23
Super Bonus Question in Arithmetic Agility

$$4 + 11 \times 5 - 66 - 8\frac{1}{2} = \frac{1}{2}$$

24
The Story of Spiro

1. Theodore

2. Not exactly a household word

3. Effete

4. Impudent snobs

5. Elite

6. Des Moines

7. "You've seen one slum, you've seen em all"

8. Polack

9. Fat Jap

10. Squishy soft

● **Who the Hell Was Charlotte Moorman?** World's best-known topless cellist

25
Music: Take 25

1. Their Soldier Boy; the Shirelles

2. The Beach Boys ("I Wish They All Could Be California Girls")

3. The Mamas and the Papas ("California Dreamin'")

4. Bob Dylan

5. Jimmy Webb

6. Dion, the Belmonts, "The Wanderer"

7. *Switched-On Bach* (Extra credit: Walter Carlos)

8. A. Sly and the Family Stone
B. Big Brother and the Holding Company
C. Canned Heat
D. The Grateful Dead
E. Creedence Clearwater Revival
F. Butterfield Blues Band
G. The Lovin' Spoonful
H. The Who
I. The Mothers of Invention
J. Gary Lewis and the Playboys

9. Nothing

10. "Louie, Louie"

11. That he had died and a double was making his personal appearances (an intriguing, and possibly true, notion)

12. "Save the Last Dance for Me"

13. Bill Graham

14. Erich Leinsdorf, Charles Munch

15. Duke Ellington

16. Igor Stravinsky

17. She redid it with the name "I Am Eleanor Rigby"

18. One of the U.S. marines who was at Iwo Jima for the raising of the flag during World War II

19. Little White Dove ("Oomba-tooka, oomba-tooka")

20. Pablo Casals

21. Bossa nova

22. "Desafinado"

23. Hank Ballard

24. Sitar, George Harrison, Ravi Shankar

25. Ticky-tacky (and they all looked just the same)

● **Who the Hell Was Rudi Dutschke?**
German socialist student leader, known as Red Rudi

26
The Letter N

1. BERLIN

2. (Lyndon) JOHNSON

3. (William) SCRANTON

4. (Janis) JOPLIN

5. (Bob) DYLAN

27
Complete the Quote

1. Hallelujah! (folk song)

2. Krishna krishna, hare hare (religious chant)

3. Children and other living things (popular poster slogan)

4. Reason together (LBJ, quoting Isaiah 1:18)

5. Dream! (Martin Luther King)

6. A New Frontier (JFK)

7. Satisfaction (Rolling Stones song)

8. Where do they all come from? (Beatles song "Eleanor Rigby")

9. To me! (*Laugh-In* catchline)

10. Chief! (*Get Smart* catchline)

● **Who the Hell Was Charles Garry?**
Lawyer for black militant Bobby Seale

28
Campaign Stuff

1. Richard Milhous Nixon and Henry Cabot Lodge

2. Barry Morris Goldwater and William Edward Miller

3. Hubert Horatio Humphrey and Edmund Sixtus Muskie

4. General Curtis Emerson LeMay (Extra credit: He was an Air Force general—Commander of SAC and the Air Force Chief of Staff)

5. Nelson Rockefeller

6. Quemoy and Matsu

7. B—Atlantic City

8. B—42

9. Pat Paulsen

10. Just one

● **Who the Hell Was Penelope Ashe?**
"Author" of *Naked Came the Stranger*, actually 25 journalists who wrote trash book as a hoax

29
True or False?

1. False
2. False—it was demolished
3. True
4. True
5. False—he won it in 1969 (and also in 1973 and 1975)
6. True
7. True—briefly
8. False—but he did host *Jackpot Bowling*
9. False—in fact, he wore one as he shot Oswald
10. True
11. False—he questioned the Trinity
12. True
13. True
14. True
15. True

30
In the Middle

1. Julius *J.* Hoffman
2. Lewis *B.* Hershey
3. Nicholas *DeB.* Katzenbach
4. Captain James *T.* Kirk
5. Christiaan *N.* Barnard
6. Billie *Sol* Estes
7. Robert *Strange* McNamara
8. Jorge *Luis* Borges

9. Nikita *Sergeyevich* Khrushchev
10. Cassius *Marcellus* Clay

● **Who the Hell Was Jack Rubenstein?** Jack Ruby

31
Rivers and Islands

1. The Yangtze River
2. Adam Clayton Powell
3. The Arno, in Florence
4. Martha's Vineyard
5. C—nuclear test site

32
On Stage

1. Rolf Hochhuth
2. *The Best Man*
3. He was drafted
4. *Toys, Attic*
5. *An Evening with Mike Nichols and Elaine May*
6. *The Persecution and Assassination of Jean-Paul Marat as Performed by the Inmates of the Asylum of Charenton Under the Direction of the Marquis de Sade*
7. *Mamma's Hung You in the Closet and I'm Feeling So Sad* (Extra credit: Arthur Kopit)
8. *MacBird* (Extra credit: Barbara Garson)
9. A central character of the tribe in *Hair* who's drafted and killed
10. *Man of La Mancha* ("The Impossible Dream")

33
Vowel Play

1. FRANK ZAPPA
2. *MIRANDA* v. *ARIZONA*
3. SYNGMAN RHEE
4. CHARLES DE GAULLE
5. JOHN PROFUMO

34
ID, Please

1. Friend of Puff, the Magic Dragon
2. Bespectacled poet, created by Ernie Kovacs
3. Gentleman for whose benefit Sgt. Pepper's Lonely Hearts Club Band performed
4. Hobbit, from the mind of J. R. R. Tolkien
5. Anthony Perkins role in *Psycho*

● **Who the Hell Was Valentina Tereshkova?** First woman in space

35
Sports

1. 1967; Green Bay Packers
2. Kansas City Chiefs; 35–10
3. Minnesota Fats, *The Hustler*
4. 1966 and 1968
5. Benny "Kid" Paret
6. Both took baseball's Triple Crown *and* the MVP

7. Ingemar Johansson
8. Herb Elliott
9. Lew Alcindor
10. Badminton; the K
11. A. J. Foyt
12. Detroit Lions and Baltimore Colts
13. Twice—once from the Yankees (in 1961), once from the Mets (1965)
14. Randy Matson
15. Came in last
16. The 1966 winner of the Kentucky Derby and the Preakness Stakes
17. ¾ inch
18. Staubach, Navy
    Garrett, USC
    Simpson, USC
    Davis, Syracuse
19. Don Drysdale
20. Won the Grand Slam of tennis—the four major titles—in one year, 1962
21. Arnold Palmer
22. He scored 100 points for the '76ers in one game against the Knicks; final score was 169–147, Philadelphia
23. Bruno Sammartino
24. Carroll Hardy, in the 1960 season's final week, after the Splendid Splinter's retirement had been announced
25. *Heidi*

36
Ha-Ha-Ha

1. Moby Grape
2. An electric grape
3. Because it doesn't know the words
4. You see its footprints in the Jell-O
5. It's a Tom Swifty

- **Who the Hell Was Ludvík Svoboda?** Czech president who supported Alexander Dubček's liberalization

37
The Number Game

1. 11, 12
2. 49—the 50th, for Hawaii, wasn't added until July 4
3. 20
4. A and C—86 and 99
5. 9; it belonged to retiring Ted Williams (Extra credit: The Splendid Splinter smashed a home run in his last at bat, against Baltimore)
6. 4 and 5
7. 451
8. 5
9. 2,000
10. 4 to 5 to 6
11. 300 million going in to 1960; 5 billion at the end of 1969
12. 109
13. 1313
14. 80, according to the 1966 hit song
15. 3

- **Who the Hell Was Louis Wolfson?** Florida industrialist who paid $20,000 to Supreme Court Associate Justice Abe Fortas

38
Isn't That Whatsisname?

1. Les Crane
2. Joseph Mobuto
3. Rick Nelson ("Travelin' Man")
4. Johnny Wayne and Frank Shuster
5. Mark Rudd

39
Who Died?

1. Lenny Bruce
2. Gracie Allen
3. Nat "King" Cole
4. Walt Disney
5. George "Gabby" Hayes
6. Clark Gable
7. Boris Karloff
8. Stan Laurel
9. Amos Alonzo Stagg
10. Sophie Tucker
11. Elsa Maxwell
12. Patrick
13. Oscar Hammerstein II
14. Harpo Marx
15. Emily Post
16. F. P. A.—Franklin Pierce Adams
17. Pope John XXIII

18.–20. Virgil Grissom, Edward White, Roger Chaffee

Who the Hell Was Donald Slayton? Astronaut scrubbed for heart palpitation just before a scheduled flight, 1962

40
How Did They Die?

1. Hemingway—self-inflicted gunshot wound
2. Kovacs—auto crash
3. Monroe—overdose of pills
4. Merton—freak electrocution in a train
5. Marciano—plane crash

41
Forgery Identification

B is the authentic signature of John F. Kennedy

42
Books

1. *Catch-22*
2. *Quotations from Chairman Mao Tse-tung*
3. "In a hierarchy, every employee tends to rise to his level of incompetence."
4. Oscar Levant
5. Lenny Bruce
6. Errol Flynn's

7. Sammy Davis, Jr.'s
8. *The Kandy-Kolored Tangerine-Flake Streamline Baby*
9. *Webster's Third New International Dictionary*
10. The human guinea pigs in Dr. Kenneth Cooper's exercise experiments, described in his best-selling *Aerobics*
11. John Steinbeck, 1962
12. It was President Eisenhower's memoirs of his administration
13. *Unsafe at Any Speed*, by Ralph Nader
14. Alex Portnoy's papa
15. A purported secret government report about the economic desirability of war. It was in fact a hoax (Extra credit: Leonard C. Lewin)
16. *Tropic of Cancer*, by Henry Miller; sequel: *Tropic of Capricorn*
17. *Valley of the Dolls*, by Jacqueline Susann
18. *Fanny Hill*
19. Hunter Thompson; he was beaten up when they found out what he was up to
20. *Down These Mean Streets*; Puerto Rican
21. Gerald Gardner
22. "The medium is the message" (Extra credit: Marshall McLuhan, *Understanding Media: The Extensions of Man*)
23. Glass
24. Postmaster General Arthur Summerfield, *Lady Chatterley's Lover*
25. Betty Friedan, in *The Feminine Mystique*

●**Who the Hell Was Dr. Maurice H. F. Wilkins?** Shared Nobel medicine award with James D. Watson and Francis. H. C. Crick

43
Initials

1. National Liberation Front
2. Student Nonviolent Coordinating Committee
3. Students for a Democratic Society
4. Multiple Independent Reentry Vehicle
5. Reserve Officers Training Corps
6. Conscientious Objector
7. Viet Cong
8. De-Militarized Zone
9. *That Was The Week That Was*
10. Special Executive for Counter-Terrorism, Revenge and Extortion (from the James Bond series)
11. Congress Of Racial Equality
12. Young American for Freedom
13. Youth International Party (Yippies)
14. Volunteers In Service To America (the domestic Peace Corps)
15. Liberation News Service
16. Lunar Excursion Module
17. United Network Command for Law and Enforcement
18. Technological Hierarchy for the Removal of Undesirables and the Subjugation of Humanity
19. War Resisters League
20. Free Speech Movement

44

Giant Sixties Word Find

```
L L E D U C T H O J R D A Y S O F R A G E S L E R T S N I M Y T S I R H C W E N
F O V I Z E R R T U P S Y C H E D E L I C L A N N O D E N A C I R R U H H Q C
R T E S L E R D G M S A R D O M M U O Y E H A L I C A N D L O U D Q M M U Z O
U U R C O D E D R Y H M C R A S Z Y L D A V I D B E N G U R I O N S O R T N V O
G N G O A J P O E C N O D N O B N A I L U J N J K A L M D O N K N O T T S L I L
M A R K R U D D E O T N P R S C L B I A A K I O N O B E L M O N D O L R I E H
S B E I N H A M N L T H T K A M D A C E M I C K E Y H A R G I T A Y Y D W A T N
A U E K Z A H C B L T E E A Y D R I E D I G A S T R O N A U T Z Z F R D O R N A
R R N O A L K C E I D R I R L Y A B O A L A M P Y B T P N D I D O Y O A R T A M
Z N R P L M S I R N A S H I E E H O A N O Y R Y B G Y N R F L B F D G L K H M I
N B E I R I S F E S L B Y N W A G R A B M O A N S E L W O B R E T S E H C N I U
O A V W N U B S T C I R H C T L L J D G I F N A J G E L V S T D S E R H E I Z K E
P I S T T F S A N G O N E U Q O I W E N R H S E L M A T Y U M I H G N I M A C
O Y F A N N O Y N N A T S A D B R F S G D H B C B S W D N U O U D Y K M N I T C
O B W B A F E A U H L H P T W L I L C T E T A Y R A Y R E N H S T I C O A H I R
E U S A K O C H R O S E E A I A A L Y O R A Y A R B I I R D Y K A A I R L C O E
E R L S T T E S R E I R Y O T C S D A P B O L H E L L B G E T I L V D I V O N H
A N N O A H R N O U C S T O F K T S E R I T R F V I S A T R E E B I N M M H A C
N K O T I C T J Y A A A O A W I E M G O N N A P A L M D E G B R T I A A L X F A
D A S I X D A Y W A R C N H T S I O L S D I I A E E G N I R F E H T N O Y E B
R H N M A O M M R K L T P H Q B N T L E E K C N L A R Y M O N T E R F O L D T L
E L A I S I N N A F O I L N B E E T L Y R N T T C S A L P U B C A O E F D R F E
A I M N D U B A G M G Y A A I A M O A G T O H Y Y E C C E R N W D N D L L T S S H
L L S O F Y V I K B L H C T H U A B W R N T Y Y H G H E L T D T R I V I A E T F C
A E S G T C R K N E M E C T T R L N I E F S O D P S W A P T I M M I M D I B S
C I L F H R M A N K S D D A D I E L I E L O T S I I L D L R T S A E B A O L B E
K B R E N E O S F H B P F T P F F E L R A F L E R A I G P E D K L O C N T L G A
L R A R J U L S N F Y E D N L U O B R I T L R G D N C D O S O F S T H C F M H Z
W A H F L Q J O Y M U P A R Y L A K E E S U R A L T K G O S B M A N T H U A E I
I N C H I T T Y C H I T T Y B A N G B A N G U Y E N C A O K Y S F O L A S N S L
```

Horizontal

LE DUC THO
DAYS OF RAGE
NEW CHRISTY MINSTRELS
PSYCHEDELIC
HURRICANE DONNA
DAVID BEN GURION
JULIAN BOND
DON KNOTTS

MARK RUDD
BELMONDO
BE IN
MICKEY HARGITAY
ASTRONAUT
CHESTER BOWLES
SELMA

NAPALM
SIX DAY WAR
BEYOND THE FRINGE
TRIVIA
CHITTY CHITTY BANG
BANG
NGUYEN CAO KY

Vertical

FRUG
BURN BABY BURN
KAHLIL GIBRAN
EVERGREEN REVIEW
CHARLES MANSON
DISCO
YOSSARIAN
GREEN BERET
JUDY COLLINS
CARL OGLESBY
SMOTHERS BROTHERS

PEYTON PLACE
BLACK IS BEAUTIFUL
GLORIA STEINEM
BELLBOTTOMS
BERLIN WALL
ROSEY GRIER
MILO MINDERBINDER
GULF OF TONKIN
CAM RANH BAY
PANTYHOSE
ELDRIDGE CLEAVER

GRACE SLICK
LYNDA BIRD
UNDERGROUND PRESS
ED MUSKIE
THE ANIMALS
DICK GREGORY
MAN OF LA MANCHA
HO CHI MINH TRAIL
DR STILLMAN
VIETNAMIZATION
COOL HAND LUKE

Diagonal

WATUSI
THE HUNGRY I
PAUL GOODMAN
OM

DR WELBY
MAMA CASS
NEHRU
THE REALIST

HONKY
DION
AQABA
ESHKOL

45.
What's My Line?

1. Meter maid (in Beatles song)
2. Fashion model
3. Handymen—of sorts (TV's *I'm Dickens . . . He's Fenster*)
4. Detective—of sorts (film series)
5. Host of television's *Death Valley Days*
6. Police officer ("Alice's Restaurant")
7. Sportswriter *(The Odd Couple)*
8. Coffee maven
9. Maid
10. USIA director
11. Poet
12. Physician
13. Dentist
14. Secretary to the Senate majority
15. Cops *(Car 54, Where Are You?)*

● **Who the Hell Was Lord Harlech?** British ambassador to the United States and, later, a prime Jackie suitor (name: David Ormsby-Gore)

46.
The Letter X

1. UNISEX
2. (Sandy) KOUFAX
3. PETER MAX
4. MAXICOAT
5. JIMI HENDRIX EXPERIENCE

47.
Magazines

1. The *Saturday Evening Post* folded
2. *Eros*
3. *Look* (Extra credit: William Manchester)
4. *Saturday Evening Post* (Extra credit: University of Georgia athletic director)
5. *Harper's* (Extra credit: *Atlantic* gave an issue to Dan Wakefield for "Supernation at Peace and War," an assessment of the mood of America)
● **Who the Hell Was Ross Barnett?** Mississippi governor who tried to block James Meredith from entering Ole Miss

48.
A Smattering of Crime

1. Richard Speck, Chicago
2. University of Texas at Austin, Charles Whitman
3. Charles H. Percy
4. The equivalent of $7,145,600
5. Joe Valachi
6. *La cosa nostra*
7. Frank Sinatra, Jr.
8. Red (her hair and social life attracted a lot of attention at her trial for the murder of her daughter)
9. California
10. Rudolf Abel

49.
What's Happening?

1. She's Shirley Temple Black, and she's been defeated for a seat in Congress, 1967
2. Christmas, most likely, since Bob Hope is entertaining the troops in Vietnam
3. O'Daniel the evangelist (John McGiver) is showing Joe Buck (Jon Voight) what praying is all about in *Midnight Cowboy*
4. He's Albert Sabin, and he's holding a vial of his oral vaccine against polio, which was licensed and went into general use in the early Sixties
5. It's hard to say exactly, but it's likely Katharine Hepburn and Katharine Houghton (as Christine Drayton and her daughter Joey) are discussing their upcoming dinner guest, Sidney Poitier, in *Guess Who's Coming to Dinner?*
6. That's Bill Moyers, LBJ's press secretary, frugging up a storm at a champagne dance to raise money for the Kennedy Center for the Performing Arts; some folks disapproved of his conduct
7. Does it *matter?* It's Jim Ryun, and he's about to break the world's record for the mile: 3:51.1, on June 23, 1967
8. This lovely trio, mimicking the Supremes, is singing "White Boys" in the musical *Hair*
9. Because the man on the left is booking the man on the right for second-degree perjury—that's Charles Van Doren, and the 1960 arrest grew out of earlier investigations into the fixing of television quiz shows
10. Because he's being inaugurated as the first black mayor of a Mississippi town since Reconstruction—it's Charles Evers of Fayette

50.
About Women

1. The mother of Massachusetts Governor Endicott Peabody is arrested during a 1964 Florida protest demonstration
2. Brandeis (Angela Davis)
3. Model (Christine Keeler)
4. All four (Judy Collins)
5. Don, played by Ted Bessell
● **Who the Hell Was Albert DeSalvo?** The Boston Strangler

51.
Hidden Words

1. I NEARLY WORSHIP PIES MADE WITH TART APPLES.
2. A MORATORIUM IS AN ANTI-WAR HOLIDAY, ISN'T IT?
3. IT TAKES TWO TO CHANGE A LIGHT BULB? JERK!
4. A BANANA PALM? MUST BE THE FRUIT OF YOUR IMAGINATION.
5. THEY MET AT A COLUMBIA FRAT PARTY, WHERE GOOD ROCK WAS PLAYED.

6. THAT MAN'S ON MY "BAD GUY" LIST . . . AND EVERYBODY ELSE'S.

7. GIVE THE FLY A SWAT, TSAR NICHOLAS!

8. A LAUGH? AN 'OI-OI-OI' WOULD BE MORE LIKE IT.

9. MILTON . . . FUNNY MILTON . . . KIND MILTON . . . THEY CALLED HIM 'MR. TELEVISION'.

10. WE SAY 'OF COURSE' IN AMERICA. THEY SAY 'NATÜRLICH' IN GERMANY.

● **Who the Hell Was Shorty Powers?** The voice of mission control; announced the countdowns at Cape Canaveral, including the one for Alan Shepard's pioneer space flight in *Freedom 7*

52
Friendly Animals

1. Macaroni
2. *101 Dalmatians*
3. R. Crumb, the underground cartoon king
4. Checkers; cocker spaniel
5. Arnold
6. Him and Her
7. French poodle (Extra credit: blue; Charles le Chien)
8. "Tie Me Kangaroo Down, Sport" (by Rolf Harris)
9. Mr. Ed
10. Ham
11. Flipper
12. Pigasus

13. Ana (for Anaheim, Calif.)
14. In your tank (according to the Esso ads)
15. "The Lion Sleeps Tonight"

53
Music: Take 20 More

1. Dominique
2. Velvet
3. A hootenanny
4. The Locomotion (she's Little Eva)
5. Jim Morrison, lead of The Doors (Extra credit: Miami Beach)
6. Alice
7. E—*Dylan Goes Home* is the phony
8. Petula Clark
9. Camp Grenada
10. Brian Epstein
11. A man and a woman
12. Melina Mercouri
13. 98.6
14. Thelonious Monk (with an "ou")
15. The Four Seasons asked Sherry (Extra credit: Bob Gaudio, Tommy deVito, leader Frankie Valli, and Joe Long)
16. A Willie or a Sam (so she had only Henrys—eight of them, in fact, according to the Herman's Hermits ditty "Henry VIII")
17. The Righteous Brothers (Extra credit: Bobby Hatfield and Bill Medley)
18. The Fugs
19. Bobby Lewis
20. That's right: The Who

● **Who the Hell Was Joseph Gargan?** A Kennedy cousin

54
Colors

1. *The Pink Panther*
2. Blue Meanies (from *Yellow Submarine*)
3. "I-B T-W Yellow P-D Bikini"
4. "White Rabbit"
5. S&H green stamps

55
Strikes, Protests, Riots, Etc.

1. Woolworth's (Extra credit: All asked for coffee)
2. C—to restrict solicitation . . .
3. The 63-page manifesto written by University of Michigan student Tom Hayden and presented at the primordial SDS meeting at Port Huron, Mich., in June 1962. It called for "the establishment of a democracy of individual participation"
4. Mayor of Newark during the 1967 riots
5. Defendant Bobby Seale raised such a fuss in the courtroom that he ·was first gagged and shackled to a chair, then separated for his own trial. Eight minus one leaves seven
6. You probably got Abbie Hoffman, Jerry Rubin, and Tom Hayden right away. Rennie Davis and David Dellinger might have taken a little longer. Then come Lee Weiner and John Froines, even harder to remember than Doc and Bashful (Grumpy was the judge)

7. Bobby Seale's 33rd

8. Fort Lauderdale was for the kids; St. Augustine had the beach-busting

9. Daniel Cohn-Bendit

10. American Indians took Alcatraz (Extra credit: They threw a Thanksgiving feast there)

- **Who the Hell Was Rufus Youngblood?** Secret Service agent who pushed LBJ to the floor of the limousine after JFK was shot

56
Words from Our Sponsors

1. Noxzema
2. Rapid Shave
3. Tornado (Ajax)
4. You, Baby
5. The Dodge Rebellion
6. Excedrin headaches
7. "Do it myself!" (Anacin)
8. Winemaker (Italian Swiss Colony)
9. Silly
10. Burma-Shave; it was the last year Burma-Shave signs were raised on the nation's highways
11. Avis v. Hertz (the question was, whose were cleaner?)
12. Avis, Hertz, No. 1
13. Contac
14. Tareyton cigarettes
15. Chateau Martin wine

57
What Do They Have in Common?

1. Chamberlain played Dr. Kildare, Edwards played Dr. Ben Casey

2. Played the Dynamic Duo in the *Batman* TV series

3. Both were underground newspapers, Great Speckled Bird in Atlanta and The Kaleidoscope in Madison, Wis.

4. Both couples were divorced in 1962

5. All were Heisman Trophy winners

6. They went to North Vietnam together on a "fact-finding mission"

7. All were aliases of James Earl Ray

8. Woods was Nixon's secretary, Lincoln was Kennedy's

9. All were occupied by student protestors

10. The second name Jo: Bobbie Jo, Billie Jo, Betty Jo

- **Who the Hell Was Louis Washkansky?** South African grocer and first successful heart transplant recipient

58
The Supreme Test

1. States and localities may not require public school children to pray or read the Bible

2. Madalyn Murray (later O'Hair), the professional atheist

3. Felix Frankfurter, Tom Clark, Charles Whittaker, Arthur Goldberg, Abe Fortas

4. 78

5. Clement Haynsworth and G. Harrold Carswell

- **Who the Hell Was Sarah Hughes?** Federal judge who administered oath of office to LBJ on plane from Dallas

59
Who Said?

1. A—President Kennedy

2. E—President Kennedy (on missiles in Cuba)

3. B—Pope Paul VI

4. D—Martin Luther King

5. George Romney (in explaining his early support of the Vietnam war)

6. Noam Chomsky (in *Syntactic Structures*)

7. David Eisenhower (on leaving the White House)

8. Allan Sherman

9. Arte Johnson (of *Laugh-In*)

10. Mrs. John Connally (to JFK the day of the shooting)

11. Madame Nhu (referring to flaming suicides of protest)

12. Robin (Batman's friend)

13. Charles de Gaulle

14. JFK

15. JFK

16. LBJ (in his first address to Congress as president)

17. Mayor Richard J. Daley

18. Adam Clayton Powell

19. Elijah Muhammad

20. Nguyen Cao Ky (South Vietnam's No. 2)

21. General Westmoreland

22. Bobby Kennedy (paraphrasing a line from the George Bernard Shaw play *Back to Methuselah*)

23. Neil Armstrong, on stepping on the moon, right after he intoned: "That's one small step for a man . . ."

24. Abbie Hoffman

25. George Wallace, 1963

26. H. Rap Brown

27. White House aide Jack Valenti

28. George Wallace

29. Barry Goldwater

30. JFK

60
One Little Word

1. Plastics

2. Water

3. Yale

4. Multiversity

5. Pregnant

6. C—Corfam

7. Apple

8. Telstar

9. Teletype (Extra credit: He tied for second—Vassily Smyslov won)

10. Daughter

11. *Barbra*

12. Destruction

13. Happiness

14. Vassar

15. Romania (1969, Nixon)

16. Marines

17. *Finie*

18. Mace

19. Fastback

20. Alone (Extra credit: *The Gipsy Moth IV*)

● **Who the Hell Was Dr. Howard Levy?** Antiwar Army doctor convicted of promoting disloyalty and disobeying orders for refusing to train Green Beret medics in dermatology

61
ING

1. RINGO (Starr)

2. (Rita) TUSHINGHAM

3. HAPPENING

4. SING ALONG (with Mitch Miller)

5. LING-TEMCO-VOUGHT

62
Quick Associations

1. Paris peace talks, at which it was a bone of contention

2. Andy Warhol, who was her pal

3. Linda Fitzpatrick, who was found murdered with him in New York's East Village

4. Susan Sontag, who wrote an essay about it

5. Richard Nixon, who belonged to the law firm

6. *Who's Afraid of Virginia Woolf?*, in which that game was suggested by Elizabeth Taylor

7. The Kennedys, about whom he wrote

8. Ruth Buzzi, of *Laugh-In*

9. The birth control pill, which he promoted

10. The Addams Family, who owned it

11. New Orleans DA Jim Garrison, who accused him of being mixed up in the JFK assassination

12. Barry Goldwater, about whom the commercial was written, and LBJ, in whose behalf it was aired

13. James Forman, who made them

14. Napoleon Solo of *The Man From U.N.C.L.E.*, about the two agents

15. The New York World's Fair, which took it as its symbol

63
Author! Author!

1. Victor Lasky
2. Bob Hope
3. John Barth
4. Johnny Carson
5. Dan Greenburg
6. Jessica Mitford
7. Gael Greene
8. Rachel Carson
9. Peg Bracken
10. Harper Lee

- **Who the Hell Was Barry Sadler?** Special Forces staff sergeant who wrote and recorded "The Ballad of the Green Berets"

64
Openers

1. *Cat's Cradle,* by Kurt Vonnegut
2. *Rabbit, Run,* by John Updike
3. *Herzog,* by Saul Bellow
4. *An American Dream,* by Norman Mailer
5. *The Life and Loves of Mr. Jiveass Nigger,* by Cecil Brown

- **Who the Hell Was Louis Abolafia?** Naked Presidential candidate, 1968 (lost)

65
About Names

1. Ernesto
2. Levi (Extra credit: Gallagher)
3. Walt Whitman (Extra credit: Eugene Victor Debs)
4. Thant was his *only* name (U is a Burmese honorific)
5. Hubert
6. Travers
7. Joseph
8. Ornette
9. Don
10. Lurleen
11. Mary Corita Kent
12. David Dean Rusk
13. It's J. R. R. Tolkien's first three names
14. McDonald (as in Fishwich)
15. Abbott H. Hoffman
16. Conrad
17. Marjorie
18. Nazerman
19. Nina
20. Andrew John (Extra credit: Woodhouse)

66
Assassination Minutiae

1. Left
2. B—Parkland Memorial
3. D—rose 32 points
4. The Lorraine
5. D—supporting a garbage collectors' strike
6. D—Italy
7. The Ambassador, in Los Angeles, where he was celebrating a win in the state primary
8. Bishara
9. Jockey
10. Atlanta (Extra credit: South View Cemetery)

- **Who the Hell Was Candy Mossler?** Acquitted in Miami of murdering her husband, Jacques

67
Song Fragments

1. "Light My Fire"
2. "Mrs. Robinson"
3. "Talk to the Animals"
4. "When I'm Sixty-Four"
5. "Sealed with a Kiss"
6. "A Hard Rain's A-Gonna Fall"
7. "The Times They Are A-Changin'"
8. "Don't Think Twice, It's All Right"
9. "Lay, Lady, Lay"
10. "Hey, Mr. Tambourine Man"

68
A Half Quiz

I shall not seek, and I will not accept, the nomination of my party for another term as your president'"(LBJ's announcement that he would not enter the '68 race)

- **Who the Hell Was Mortimer Caplin?** IRS commissioner

69
Black Studies

1. Little
2. Thurgood Marshall, replacing Clark on the U.S. Supreme Court (Extra credit: He was Solicitor General of the United States)
3. Carl Rowan
4. James Brown, loud ("Say It Loud")
5. Julia; widow (Extra credit: Cory)
6. *My Name, Country, Next Time*
7. The Bill Cosby character on *I Spy* (Robert Culp was Robinson)
8. Imamu Amiri Baraka
9. Medgar Evers
10. Malcolm X was killed

70
Fill in the Blanks

1. Back; plane
2. *Dolce Vita*
3. Billy Rose

4. Lyndon Johnson
5. First Lieutenant
6. Robert Frost; JFK
7. *Acid Test*
8. Patrice
9. Filthy (students ran around with dirty words painted on their foreheads and a good time was had by all)
10. Gone

- **Who the Hell Was Viola Liuzzo?** Civil rights worker shot to death between Selma and Montgomery, 1965

71
Talk to the Stars

1. "What's it all about, Alfie?" (That's Michael Caine, in the movie called *Alfie*)
2. Mr. C.
3. God (It's Tevye, as portrayed by Herschel Bernardi in *Fiddler on the Roof*)
4. Cecilia (in the song of that name, by Simon and Garfunkel)
5. "Ommmmmmmm!" (It's Allen Ginsberg, well-known Om chanter)

- **Who the Hell Was James Farmer?** CORE leader

72
In a Family Way

1. Brother
2. Sister-in-law
3. Frank and Nancy Sinatra, father and daughter

4. Father and daughter
5. John Steinbeck IV

- **Who the Hell Was Linda LeClair?** Barnard coed censured for living with her boyfriend

73
More Sports—for the Hardcore

1. Tracy Stallard of the Red Sox
2. Rod Carew
3. Six
4. D—176
5. B—288
6. A—Alabama
7. Chicago Black Hawks
8. Army
9. Arthur Ashe (Extra credit: Tom Okker)
10. 1960—Pirates over Yankees, 4–3
    1962—Yankees over Giants, 4–3
    1964—Cardinals over Yankees, 4–3
    1966—Orioles over Dodgers, 4–0
    1968—Tigers over Cardinals, 4–3
11. Joe Pepitone (whose error set up the Dodgers' winning run)
12. His team, Baltimore, lost the game 2 to 1 (Barber was relieved, with one out to go in the ninth, by Stu Miller, who lost the game on a wild pitch and an error)

13. Ernie Davis

14. Washington

15. Jim Gentile; 5

16. Thirteen

17. Steve Carlton of St. Louis, in 1969

18. It was 1962, in Chicago's Wrigley Field (Extra credit: 9–4, American)

19. Rick Barry (with 2,775 points, for a 35.6 average)

20. They're the Sixties winners (in order) of the American League Rookie-of-the-Year Award

21. C—Roberto Clemente

22. All three, if you count the 1963 tie between McCovey and Aaron

23. Charlie Pasarell

24. Yelberton Abraham Tittle

25. Bailey Howell and Walter Dukes

● **Who the Hell Was Michael Lindsay-Hogg?** Director of Beatles film *Let It Be*

74
Explain

1. If you were in the northeastern United States on Nov. 9, 1965, you were in darkness: that's the date of the Great Blackout. The question became one of the most popular of the decade, along with "Where were you when JFK was shot?" and "Hey, baby, wha's happenin'?"

2. That was Barry Goldwater's mock-chemistry campaign name in 1964: Au for gold, H_2O for water. You read it on bumper stickers

3. David Brinkley didn't cross the lines, Chet Huntley did, because, he said, he didn't like being represented by a union made up mostly of "actors, singers, comedians, and jugglers" (Burning question left unanswered: During the strike, did David and Chet say goodnight to each other?)

4. "Win this one for Ike!" That's Richard Nixon speaking at the end of the 1968 convention, as Eisenhower lay critically ill in Walter Reed Army Hospital

5. That was LBJ, upon seeing a portrait of himself (Extra credit: the artist, Peter Hurd)

75
Just Eyes

1. Jim Nabors   2. Roy Wilkins

3. Elliott Gould   4. William F. Buckley, Jr.

5. Hugh Downs   6. Adlai Stevenson

7. Spencer Tracy   8. Whitney Young, Jr.

9. Helen Reddy

10. Hubert Humphrey

15. John F. Kennedy

16. Buddy Hackett

11. Flip Wilson

12. Rose Marie

17. John L. Lewis

18. Mia Farrow

13. Elizabeth Taylor

14. Fred MacMurray

19. Gale Gordon

20. Lassie

●**Who the Hell Was Leonard Weinglass?** Co-counsel for the Chicago Seven

76
Special Mystery Photo

Nikita Khrushchev's daughters: Julia Gontar, Jelena Khrushchev, and Rada Adzmubei

77
A Hairy Test

1. Bess Myerson
2. Suzy Parker
3. Julie Andrews
4. Natalie Wood
5. Audrey Hepburn
6. Wilhelmina
7. Donna Reed
8. Charlotte Ford
9. Edie Adams
10. Irene Dunne

●**Who the Hell Was Peter Best?** Replaced by Ringo as Beatles drummer

78
Health and Welfare

1. As a sedative and sleeping pill
2. *Human Sexual Response*
3. Psychiatric case histories
4. His gall bladder (Remember the scar he showed off?)

5. She went to seek an immediate legal abortion, which she had been denied at home despite her fear that her baby would be born deformed because of thalidomide (Extra credit: Sherri Finkbine)

6. The laetrile of its day, Krebiozen was an "anti-cancer drug" the government said was worthless. Some patients said it kept them alive

7. *Calories Don't Count* (his 1961 book)

8. Dr. Stillman

9. Zen Macrobiotics

10. Luther Terry

● **Who the Hell Was Claudia Johnson?** Lady Bird

79
Multiple Choice

1. B—the Rolling Stones
2. D—Winston Churchill
3. B—New Hampshire
4. B—*Minnow*
5. C—meat abstinence would be optional
6. C—madison
7. C—Tallahatchie
8. C—Resurrection City
9. C—Blair General
10. A—County General
11. A—Stokely
12. A—Christmas
13. D—tried to contact his dead son and later died following a fall in the Judean desert

14. E—Mark Clark
15. B—F. Lee Bailey
16. A—the Nobel Prize
17. C—Garden City, Kan.
18. A—the Woodstock Music and Art Fair
19. E—Spanish
20. C—contempt (William Kunstler)
21. B—Annette and Frankie
22. B—Venus
23. Would you believe D—*Get Smart?*
24. B—plane crash (Extra credit: Southern Rhodesia)
25. D—the seventh house (according to "Aquarius," the song from *Hair*)

● **Who the Hell Was J. D. Tippitt?** Dallas cop murdered as he tried to question Lee Oswald

80
Odd One Out

1. F—*Baby*
2. B—James Dean (he died in the Fifties)
3. B—Jack was older
4. D—*Venus de Milo*
5. B—Bertrand Russell
6. D—Fox's U-Bet
7. D—Romania stayed home
8. B—"Shimmy Shimmy Koko Bop" (it was a hit in the Fifties)
9. D—Nixon's the one
10. Sorry, they all did

81
And Then They Grew Up

1. Donny Osmond
2. John F. Kennedy, Jr.
3. Ron Howard, who played Opie on *The Andy Griffith Show*
4. Dino (Martin), Desi (Arnaz) and Billy
5. Larry Matthews as Richie Petrie on *The Dick Van Dyke Show* with Dick and Mary Tyler Moore (Extra credit: His middle name, like Charles Foster Kane's sled, was Rosebud)

82
Farewells

1. 1962 (Extra credit: Cincinnati)
2. So his son Ramsey could cleanly assume the post of attorney general
3. H.M.S. *Queen Mary*
4. The TV show *What's My Line* was finally laid to rest
5. Nasser
6. C—fled to Italy
7. Algiers
8. Hong Kong (Extra credit: a joke about a water closet)
9. Wilt Chamberlain
10. Because the brass above him chose to show reruns of *I Love Lucy* and *The Real McCoys* instead of Senate hearings on Vietnam

● **Who the Hell Was Valerie Solanas?** Militant feminist who shot Andy Warhol in the stomach

83
The Honors Test

1. Braddock
2. Raoul; blond
3. Ho Chi Minh
4. Bob Dylan
5. Hilton Plaza
6. A—his thighbone
7. Barbara Jane Mackle
8. Copenhagen's bronze, *The Little Mermaid*, on a rock on the Langelinie harbor promenade was beheaded
9. "Lisa and David"
10. Rutgers University (Extra credit: Colombia)
11. President Johnson, speaking in the presidential jet just after being sworn in on Nov. 22, 1963 (it was his first executive order)
12. Janet Travell
13. M.
14. Room 604
15. Cherry brandy
16. The title tells all: *Werewolf in a Girls' Dormitory*
17. "I-Feel-Like-I'm-Fixin'-to-Die-Rag" (sung by Country Joe and the Fish)
18. Avanti
19. A—Herschel
20. The soprano who dubbed songs for Natalie Wood in *West Side Story* and Audrey Hepburn in *My Fair Lady*, among others

84
But . . .

1. Denise Ann Darvall's heart was given to Louis Washkansky by Christiaan Barnard and team in Cape Town, South Africa
2. "And so, my fellow Americans"
3. "Just think how much you're going to be missing"
4. Phoned the FBI and threatened to kill President Johnson
5. Sixth (all the way at the right)

● **Who the Hell Was Emmett Grogan?** Haight-Ashbury leader, proponent of free this and that for all

85

For High Honors

1. Jack Weinberg of Berkeley's Free Speech Movement; he was 24 then

2. New Delhi; to scatter the ashes of her late third husband, an Indian Communist, in the Ganges River

3. James T. Ralph

4. "Ozzie Rabbit"

5. The medical officer at Woodstock

6. The first commander of *Star Trek's* Starship Enterprise, before Captain Kirk

7. Juanita Duggan Roberts and George G. Burkley

8. A Jackie Gleason game show on television in 1961 (it was an instant bomb)

9. Honduras won, 1–0, in overtime

10. Herman Cohen; he created the teen-age-monster fad of the late Fifties, with *I Was a Teenage Werewolf* and *I Was a Teenage Frankenstein*

11. Soeur Luc-Gabrielle

12. The Carousel Club and the Vegas Club

13. It was said to be the tree that inspired Joyce Kilmer's poem "Trees"

14. September 14

15. Edwin Goodgold and Dan Carlinsky

- **Who the Hell Was Abigail Folger?** Young coffee heiress murdered with Sharon Tate in Beverly Hills, 1969

86

Final Potpourri

1. *A Prophetic Minority*

2. Ken (1961), Midge (1963), Christie (1968)

3. Mickey Mantle won it three times—1956, 1957, 1962

4. They *The Fifth Dimension*

5. Birmingham (Extra credit: Eugene)

6. George Hamilton

7. Just one

8. Nixon won on November 5; Julie married David on December 22

9. Louisette Bertholle and Simone Beck

10. "Breakin' up is hard to do"

11. *Rush to Judgment*

12. Mrs. Robinson (from the Simon and Garfunkel song)

13. Edwin

14. Rod McKuen (who poeticized about it)

15. The artichoke

- **Who the Hell Was Sam the Plumber?** New Jersey Mafia figure, real name Simone Rizzo DeCavalcante (not to be confused with Josephine the Plumber Lady)

- Scattered through this Answer section are the answers for 50 Who the Hell Was . . . ? questions. Award yourself 10 points for each correct answer and write the total here.

Score_____**(max. 500)**
Carry total to page xii.

Photo Credits

(Page columns A, B, C from left)

Wide World: i, v(left) 1(A)(B-top)(B-bottom), 2(A)(B), 3(C)(D), 5, 8(A)(B), 12(B-bottom), 14(B-top), 18(A)(B-top), 19(A)(B), 28, 34, 37(A-top)(B-top)(C), 38(C), 39(A)(B), 40, 42(B), 44, 46(B), 50(A), 60(A)(B)(C), 61(A-top), 62(C-top)(C-bottom), 64(B), 65(A-top), 67(B), 71(B), 74, 75(A), 77(A-top left, right)(A-middle)(B-bottom)(C-top)(C-middle), 84(A)(B), 85(B-bottom), 86(A), 89(A), 90(A-bottom), 94(A)(B), 106, 116(A)(B), 118(B-top)

UPI: 3(B), 12(B)(C-top), 14(A-bottom), 16, 18(B-bottom)(C), 36, 38(A), 42(A), 46(A), 47(A-bottom)(B), 63(B-top)(B-bottom), 67(A), 71(A), 73(A), 76, 81(C), 85(B-top), 91(A), 93(B), 100, 107(A)(B), 108, 109(B-top), 113(B)

Rutgers: 114, 118(A)

Yale University News Bureau: 2(C), 3(A-top)

Columbia University News Office: 112(B)

Glassboro State College: 6(C)

Don Kechely: 117(A)

Steve Rose, LNS: 12(A)

U.S. Army: 39(C)

NASA: 48(C)

Dick Corten: 23(C), 64(A)

Cover: Twiggy, Che Guevara, Martin Luther King—all Wide World